NEW HODDER ENGLISH

Sue Hackman • Alan Howe • Patrick Scott

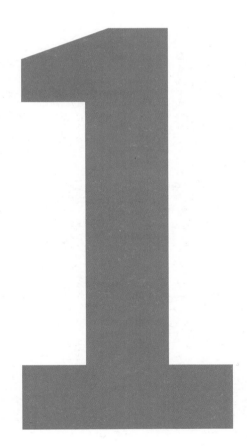

1

Hodder & Stoughton

A MEMBER OF THE HODDER HEADLINE GROUP

ACKNOWLEDGEMENTS

The publishers would like to thank the following contributors:

Cristina Bennett	– Unit One, *Storytelling*
Karen Blake and Lynette Newman	– Unit Two, *Personal Language File*
Jean Moore and John Catron	– Unit Three, *The Mystery of the Lost Children*
John Rowley and David Watkinson	– Unit Four, *Quests and Journeys*
Bill Turner	– Unit Five, *The Snake Stone*
Kevin Eames	– Unit Six, *Our Changing Language*
Bernadette Fitzgerald	– Unit Seven, *Poetry in Performance*

Edited by Kevin Eames

Copyright Text:
Unit One: *Jim Henson's The Storyteller*, Anthony Minghella, ©1988 Henson Associates, Inc; extracts from *Sir Gawain and the Green Knight*, as read by Hugh Lupton, *Midwinter Tales* audio Cassette (audio cassettes available from The Company of Storytellers, 8 Church Terrace, Aylsham, Norfolk); 'The Squire's Bride' from *The Woman in the Moon*, ©1984 James Riordan, Hutchinson; *Mind Your Language 1* ©1988, Palmer & Bunton, published by Oliver & Boyd; *Signposts to Spelling* ©1978, Pollock, reprinted by permission of Heinnemann Educational Publishers, a division of Reed Educational & Professional Publishing Ltd; *Spelling 9-13* ©1996 Sue Hackman & Liz Trickett, Hodder & Stoughton Educational; 'Teacher Said' © Judith Nicholls, from *Magic Mirror*, Faber & Faber Ltd; *Northern Lights* © Philip Pullman, Scholastic; 'Who's Afraid of the Big Bad Wolf' from *Young Explorer* Magazine Oct-Dec 1996, Universal Publishing Service, Malaysia; 'Mirror Writing' by Karen Adriaanse, from *The Initial Certificate in Teaching Basic Communication Skills*, Session 3 (1998), reproduced by kind permission of The Basic Skills Agency; *Captain Corelli's Mandolin* © Louis de Bernières, published by Secker & Windus; *The Cats of Seroster*, ©1984 Robert Westall, Macmillan Children's Books; *Momo* ©1985 Michael Ende, Doubleday Inc; *The Hobbit* ©1937 J R R Tolkien, HarperCollins; *The Neverending Story* ©1985 Michael Ende, Penguin; *Enchanters' End Game*, ©1985 David Eddings, Transworld Publishers Ltd, all rights reserved; 'To See the Rabbit', © Alan Brownjohn; *The Snake-stone* ©1995, Berlie Doherty, published by HarperCollins; *Preparing for a Reunion* © Julia Feast, Michael Marwood, Sue Seabrook, Elizabeth Webb, published by and reproduced with permission of The Children's Society; dictionary entry taken from *Collins School Dictionary*; 'Skipping Song', ©1985 Gareth Owen from *Song of the City*, HarperCollins; 'Rope Rhyme', © Eloise Greenfield; 'Macavity The Mystery Cat' from *Old Possum's Books of Practical Cats*, ©1939 T. S. Eliot, ©1967 renewed by Esme Valerie Eliot, Faber & Faber; 'The Looker-on', © Frank Kendon, from *The Cherry Minder*, J M Dent; 'They Held up a Stone', © Dannie Abse, from *The Hebrew of Amir*, Oxford University Press, by permission of Sheila Land Associates; 'You' from *Igbo Traditional Verse* © Nwamife Publishers; 'Sunny Market Song', © James Berry from *When I Dance*, Penguin.

Copyright Photographs:
p38, Titanic, © Denis Cochrane Collection/ E.T.Archive; p44, Wolf Hybrid, RSPCA Photolibrary © Colin Seddon; p90, Indiana Jones, © Topham Picturepoint; p102, rabbit in field, © Jean-Paul Ferrero/Ardea London Ltd; p106 (r), photo of boy and girl on bench, Dundee Art Galleries; p130/131, Maps taken from *The Cambridge Encyclopedia of the English Language* ©1995 David Crystal, published by Cambridge University Press; p137(l), English Abbot (scribe) © The Art Archive/British Library; p137 (r), William Caxton © The Art Archive; p138 & 144, Shakespeare © N.P.G. London; p154-5, The Charge of the Light Brigade; Balaclava, by Richard Caton Woodville © Private Collection/ Bridgeman Art Library.

Every effort has been made to trace copyright holders of material reproduced in this book. Any rights not acknowledged here will be acknowledged in subsequent printings if notice is given to the publisher.

Orders: please contact Bookpoint Ltd, 130 Milton Park, Abingdon, Oxon OX14 4SB. Telephone: (44) 01235 400414, Fax: (44) 01235 400454. Lines are open from 9.00am - 6.00pm, Monday to Saturday, with a 24 hour message answering service. Email address: orders@bookpoint.co.uk

British Library Cataloguing in Publication Data
A catalogue record for this title is available from the British Library.

ISBN   0 340 77536 X

First published 2001
Impression number   10 9 8 7 6 5 4 3 2
Year   2004   2003   2002   2001
Copyright © 2001 Sue Hackman, Alan Howe and Patrick Scott

Design by Mind's Eye Design, Lewes. Printed in Italy for Hodder & Stoughton Educational, a division of Hodder Headline plc, 338 Euston Road, London NW1 3BH.

INTRODUCTION

Welcome to *New Hodder English*. This course book and its two companions represent a quality English curriculum for Key Stage 3 (S1–3). It addresses objectives in the National Strategy English Framework for Key Stage 3 and full Teacher Guidance and Mapping Charts are available for download FREE at www.hodderenglish.co.uk. It promotes an interactive teaching approach which is essential to raising standards and meets the demands of the revised National Curriculum Programme of Study (and Scottish 5-14 guidelines) without compromising on range, quality literature and a progressive ethos.

STRUCTURE OF THE BOOK

The book is comprised of seven units, which are arranged to establish, revisit and consolidate key skills. Over the period of a year, all teaching points are revisited in new contexts. This course provides a full curriculum for those who wish to use it that way, but it is also a flexible resource. The units can be enhanced with texts and materials that schools have found successful, or organised around existing programmes of work.

LANGUAGE SKILLS

Language skills are developed in three ways. Firstly, each coursebook contains a unit devoted directly to language skills, and all the others take as their topic a linguistic or literary focus. Secondly, every opportunity is taken to teach language conventions at the time they are required in context. At these points, the conventions are taught directly and explicitly. Thirdly, it is assumed that teachers will continue to support pupils by giving them feedback on the detail of their writing, and specific support is provided in the Help Boxes.

STRUCTURE OF UNITS

Each unit is prefaced by a statement of aims, so that pupils have a sense of why they are undertaking the work. The activities in the unit are designed to introduce new skills and knowledge, consolidate the key points of learning and then to explore and develop these key points. Most activities can be undertaken individually or in groups. As much room as possible has been left for teachers to organise the activities in their own way. Each unit concludes with suggestions for further work to extend the more able.

PROGRESSION

The coursebook has been designed to interest and develop pupils of a wide range of ability, and most schools will find it suitable for mixed ability classes. The intention is to provide a motivating and accessible way in to the full curriculum for all pupils, and to establish, consolidate and extend a handful of key learning points in each unit.

ASSESSMENT

Teachers should continue to use their usual patterns of assessment and recording, though the organisation of the course in units does lend itself to periodic review and a focus for assessment. Each unit contains focal writing assignments which will form one important strand of assessment. Importantly, teachers will be able to assess how far pupils have learnt new ideas and been able to use them in their own reading, writing and speaking. In the end, this is the only real test of effective teaching and learning.

CONTENTS

UNIT ONE

Storytelling

'We are all storytellers, if only we are given the chance...'

In this unit, you will discover the art of storytelling: what makes a story and what makes a storyteller. You will develop skills as:

SPEAKERS AND LISTENERS

by discussing with other students in your group what you think
    makes a story work
by becoming a storyteller yourself, telling stories you know or have
    invented to a variety of groups

READERS

by reading a selection of traditional stories from different cultures
by selecting features of these stories for discussion

WRITERS

by keeping a journal in which you review your progress as a storyteller
by making notes, lists and charts to show what you have discovered
by writing your own folk tale

Turn the page and read the story of a storyteller, a 'weaver of dreams', who one day cooks for the King's cook...

A STORY SHORT

Yesterday I was telling a marvellous tale of how the moon became round and suddenly, as I reached the best bit, I couldn't remember what came next. I still can't. And staring at the expectant faces...I thought: what will I do when there are no more stories in me? When the well runs dry? What use a Storyteller without stories?

Yes, yesterday I forgot a story and that is why I went straight out and gave my supper to a beggar. Now of course, this will strike fools as foolish and wise men as wise. A fool eats his last potato. A wise man plants it. Apart from which, everyone knows beggars are never what they seem. There was a time when I myself was forced to beg. A bad time, a cold time, when a great hunger was on the land and only the rich had bellies. And so it was that one morning I found myself in sight of a Palace and in smell of a kitchen, drawn there by the sweet sweet aroma of roasting. I came to a door and stood deciphering each strand of scent...duck, goose, lamb. Mmmmm. And just about to knock was I when a raggedy character came flying through the air,

launched by the boot of a round, red Cook.

'Out,' bellowed the Cook to the bewildered Beggar, 'and stay out of my kitchen!' Then his hot face swivelled and noticed me, no prince myself, in my torn green cloak of patches and cheeks sucked in with hunger.

Before he could bring his boot to my own threadbare pants, I introduced myself with a flourish.

'I have boiled men for wasting my time,' was the Cook's inhospitable reply.

I thought on this and then remarked on the wisdom of such a measure. I did not want to waste his time, I told him humbly, I simply wanted a little water to make myself some soup. And with that, I scratched a stone free from the ground and held it up. Stone Soup, I explained, polishing it on my cloak.

The Cook puffed out his cheeks. 'You can't make soup out of a stone,' he scoffed.

'Oh yes I can,' I smiled, and winked at the poor Beggar on the ground beside me. Then, bowing and scraping, I plunged into the steamy delights of the kitchen, the Beggar slipping in with me, and while the Cook filled a large pot with cold water, I beamed to the old chap. 'Master Cook is a fool,' I whispered. 'He cuts the meat and others eat,' and we watched as the pot of water was placed over the scorching flames.

'Now,' boomed the Cook, his face shining like an apple, his head wobbling pompously, 'Let's see this Stone Soup...'

With great ceremony, I dropped the stone into the water and put my ear to it, listening carefully, the Cook watching my every move with a suspicious glare. Then, satisfied, I straightened up and folded my arms. 'How long is this going to take?' demanded the Cook.

'Not long,' I assured him. 'About an hour.' With that I stuck a finger into the pot and sucked on the liquid. 'Marvellous water,' I pronounced it. And so it was that our friend the Cook stood over me for an hour as the soup boiled, while one by one all the kitchen boys gathered around us to see this marvellous recipe, a simple stone in bubbling water.

'Well?' the Cook bellowed as the hour was up.

I stirred the water with a ladle and sipped. 'MMMMMmmm!' I murmured, wearing my best smile and 'Oh yes!'
The Cook wanted a taste. 'Do you have a little salt?' I enquired, politely.

'Salt!' roared the Cook to his minions who scattered, returning with a dish.

In went the salt, in went my ladle. 'Mmmmmmmmmm!' I reported, licking my lips. 'Almost perfect,' then I allowed the smallest flicker of misgiving to cross my eyes, sharing my doubts, one cook to the next as he waited for a sip. 'Is there any stock? The tiniest drop?'

'Stock!' and the minions were off again and back with the juices in a jiff. And after stock, I needed greens, and after greens I needed potatoes, then a carrot, then an onion. In they all went, stirred round, bubbling up, my eyes darting from pot to Cook, then from Cook to the Beggar who looked on, his wise eyes twinkling with merriment.

Finally came lamb, beef, a platter of best meat. The Cook shovelled it in, until I stopped him, with a warning hand. 'Careful,' I said, gravely. 'You'll drown the soup,' and ate the last piece to prevent him from doing so. The Stone Soup was ready.

I carried the pot to the table and ladled out three bowls, the whole kitchen following behind me. We sat, Cook, Beggar, your man, and drank it down. 'Good,' pronounced the Cook, 'very good!' and had a second bowl, then a third, the Beggar and I matching him spoon for spoon. 'Stone Soup!' he muttered between each gulp, his head shaking in disbelief. 'Marvellous.' And the minions applauded, hoping for a taste.

Full to the brim, I wiped my mouth, then fetched the scalding stone out of the pot with the ladle. 'Keep this,' I said, all generous, and lobbed it into the Cook's greedy fat fingers.

He caught it eagerly and sat, happy, a man with a magic stone, until the treasure began to sizzle in his hands. 'Owwwwwwwwww!' he screamed and fell back, spilling soup, stone, plate and all, landing in a furious rage on the floor. 'Owwwwwwwwww!'

Moments later, I found myself in a sorry state, thrown to the ground in front of the Court while the beetroot Cook, hand smarting, temper erupting in spits of bile, recounted my mischief to the King. A man with a full stomach can bear a great deal. I wasn't listening to them. I was listening to the sweet gurgles of my digestion. Let them rant and rave, I thought. I was working up a fine belch. For all I knew the Cook would burst soon with his fury and that would be the end of it. Meanwhile, he seemed to be stressing each point of his tale with a sharp kick to my ribs, not very nice.

Enough, I thought, and then realised someone was speaking to me. 'Answer the King, blockhead!' bellowed the Cook. Oh dear, I looked up and saw His Majesty waiting on a reply to a question I hadn't heard. Next to him sat the Queen, her long neck twisted in a question mark, and in front of their throne, the Prince, a boy with the eyes of an imp, who carried a small stuffed toy in the shape of a teddy bear, whose head he twisted, staring at me.

'Yes,' I answered tentatively, hoping that might do.

'What is your trade, fool?' demanded the Cook, with another swipe at my sore ribs. 'It can be scratched on your gravestone.' I didn't much like the sound of this.

'I am a teller of stories,' I began, my eyes fixed on the head of the teddy bear as it twisted and twisted. 'A weaver of dreams.'

From *Jim Henson's The Storyteller* by Anthony Minghella

STORIES – WRITTEN OR SPOKEN?

Stories are an important form of communication. We read stories in books and in newspapers, we tell stories about our lives to friends on the telephone, we listen to stories in hit songs, we read poetry, write diaries and tell jokes.

THE STONE SOUP REPORT

- Taking the role of newsreader for the evening television news, write a two paragraph report about the case of the storyteller and the cook that you plan to read on tonight's news programme.

> **(Bulletin 1)**
> **The King's guards arrested a 40-year-old man this afternoon on the charge of grievous bodily harm...**

- In pairs, pick two or three paragraphs from *A Story Short*. List the similarities and differences between these paragraphs from a narrative text, and from the report which you have just written. Discuss with your partner how the differences might make you read the two types of texts in different ways. Try your ideas out, reading the two texts aloud. One of you should take the part of the storyteller, and try to make your voice sound as interesting as possible. The other should take the role of the newsreader, reading in a voice suitable for the evening news. How did the differences in the language of the narrative text and the report help you read in different voices?

- *A Story Short* is the kind of story that should be read aloud. In your group, look again at page seven. List the phrases, words and punctuation marks that help the **narrator** know what tone of voice and what actions to use.

HELP

'To narrate' means 'to tell the story of,' and so the '**narrator**' is the teller of the story. The story itself can be called the 'narrative'.

STORIES SPOKEN

Many stories such as folk tales, legends and myths, are told and retold for generations before they are written down.

HELP

Folk tale - a short story which has been traditionally told and retold (some are now written down).
Myth - a story about a supernatural being (such as a god or a horse with wings) which was once believed true by a certain set of people, and which explained how the world came to be as it is.
Legend - a story about a person (such as Robin Hood) which may be true or was once believed true.
Fable - a story which is made up to give an example of why a person should behave in a certain way, so we say it has a 'moral'.

TELLING STORIES

- Organise yourselves into groups of four and appoint a chairperson, who will also report back to the whole class when you need to share your ideas. Think about oral storytelling – telling stories aloud. What are the advantages and disadvantages of this kind of storytelling? Remember to summarise your ideas in your notebooks or journals, or on a chart.

- Now take some time to think about telling the story of something that happened to you, or to someone you know. Your story might be funny, sad, frightening or exciting. Consider how you will tell it and then tell your story to the rest of the group. Listen carefully to each member's story so that you can retell one of the stories you have heard.

- Choose one of the stories told by another group member, and imagine that you are going to tell it to a group of six-year-olds. How will you change the way it is told? What would you need to add to make the story even more interesting? Retell the story to your group as though telling it to a group of six-year-olds.

- Discuss and record your ideas about the way you told these stories. Which ones were the most interesting? What were the 'ingredients' that made them interesting?

THE ART OF STORYTELLING

The story you tell must be interesting to your audience, but the words you use and the tone of voice in which you speak are just as important. These are the tools of storytelling – they create the pictures and the atmosphere in the imagination of the listener.

IMAGES AND ATMOSPHERE

- In small groups, write down on strips of paper several different situations. For example, getting into a freezing cold bath, walking through a dark forest. Put the strips into an envelope or box and take it in turns to pick one out. Describe the scene in terms of the senses – sight, touch, smell, sound, taste.

- Discuss how some patterns of words work in stories you know. For example, why are there three little pigs, three bears, three wishes, a hundred years' sleep. What is the effect of patterns of repetition such as 'he walked and he walked and he walked', or 'what big eyes you have... what big ears you have...'?

USING YOUR VOICE

- In pairs, think of a phrase (for example, 'What did you do?') and take it in turns to say it in as many different ways as possible: screaming, excited, angry, sorrowful, smiling, frightened. You will find that the pitch of your voice varies depending on what effect you want to create – you may use a higher pitch when showing excitement than you do for happiness, a low voice for sorrow, and a very high pitch when screaming. Try putting emphasis on each of the different words in your phrase in turn: *What* did you do? What *did* you do? What did *you* do? What did you *do*?

- Tell your partner how you get to school every day. Once you've started, don't stop, just vary the speed of what you say, from slow to fast then slow again. Your partner can listen carefully and tell you what effects were created by the varied pace.

REMEMBERING A STORY

How can you remember a story you've heard, well enough to be able to tell it to someone else?

- Listen to a story that is new to you. It may be read by your teacher or a storyteller, or it may be on tape or video. Quickly tell the complete story to your group in no more than 90 seconds! You'll be surprised at how much you remember.

- Make a bone pattern of seven words which will bring back the story into your mind.

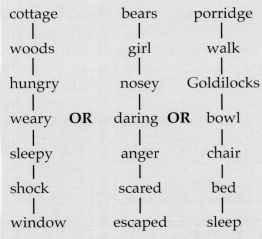

HELP

A bone pattern for the story of *Goldilocks and the Three Bears*

cottage	bears	porridge
woods	girl	walk
hungry	nosey	Goldilocks
weary **OR**	daring **OR**	bowl
sleepy	anger	chair
shock	scared	bed
window	escaped	sleep

A bone pattern is a sequence of words which follows the sequence of a story and it is a quick way of helping to keep the story fresh in your mind. Each word in the sequence brings a whole section of the story back to mind.

- Re-tell the story from the point of view of one of the characters or objects within the story. For example, how would Goldilocks tell her own story – it would probably be very different from the way it is usually told – would she be proud of what she had done? Would she be sorry? Think about how different the story would be if it was told from the viewpoint of the porridge, the chair or the bed!

WHAT THE STORYTELLERS SAY...

'...I choose a story from the many I read or hear because something of it stays with me, steps into my imagination and niggles and pesters until I take notice of it. It may be the pattern, cleverness or wit of the story, the images, symbols, strength of emotion, or all of them together. But by the time I decide to learn it, the essence of the tale is caught and I am committed to making it my own. I never learn a story word for word, but always as a series of images. If I have the image secure, the words seem to find themselves...'

Heather Sharp

'...When you have found a story you like, read it several times and let it sit around in your mind a bit. Think through the parts that interest you. What is it about and who? What happens? When the story has started to ferment in your mind, check up on what you have forgotten and start the real work of visualising the story as if you were there in person. Look around, in your imagination, breathe in the scenes, describe it all to yourself. Hear it too. What are the people in the story saying?...'

Mary Medlicott

'...Stories don't begin. We make them begin...'

Harold Rosen

'...We are all storytellers, if only we are given the chance...'

Harold Rosen

'There's no barrier between me and the listeners - no book to look down at to remind me of what to say. I look directly at my audience and the story lives in the words that I speak and in the voices I use. A story told is a story alive. Each word helps the listener build up an image ready for them to re-tell to their listeners.'

Cristina Bennett

'...in stories we, the storytellers, make endings...'

Harold Rosen

WHAT MAKES A GOOD STORYTELLER?

- Look at the comments of the storytellers on the previous two pages. Put these statements in order of importance. Select the one which you think is most important, and explain to your group why you chose it. Did the rest of the group choose the same statement, for the same reason? If not, decide as a group what the most important statement is, with reasons. Record your decisions and your reasons. Did you or anyone else change their mind? What reasons made them do that?

- Now, as a group, brainstorm and record what you have learnt so far about everything needed to be a good storyteller.

HELP

Make sure you discuss and write about:

- how a storyteller might attract their listeners' attention;
- the voice(s) of the storyteller;
- the way a storyteller might start or finish telling a story;
- any word patterns a storyteller might use to make the story come alive;
- things that have stuck in your mind about a professional storyteller if you've ever had the chance to meet one.

'A STORY ALIVE'

Now that you have looked at the important techniques of storytelling, you need to select a story and use your skills to bring it to life.

This section of the unit will help you prepare to retell a story you have chosen. Retelling a story you've heard isn't just about remembering the way a storyteller told it, it's about making it your own. You have to adapt your chosen story and add things which you think will work well, such as:

- an effective opening, to grab the listener's attention

- some detailed description to help the listeners imagine characters and places

- appropriate language to suit the time and the setting of the story, and to create atmosphere

- different voices for the different characters you introduce, keeping these going throughout your telling

- a good ending.

CHOOSE A STORY

- Choose a story you have heard or read to re-tell in your own way. It should be one you found interesting and will enjoy telling to your audience. Noting down a bone pattern and learning it will help

you to remember the events around which you will build your own version.

- Make a note of which story you have chosen, and why, in your journal.

EFFECTIVE OPENINGS

'Once upon a time when all big folks were wee ones and all lies were true..'

'Once upon a time and twice upon a time and all times together as ever I heard tell of...'

'Once upon a time, and a very good time it was, though it wasn't in my time, nor in your time, nor anyone else's time, but sometime...'

'Once upon a time when pigs spoke rhyme, and monkeys chewed tobacco, and hens took snuff to make them tough and ducks went quack, quack, o!'

FINDING AN OPENING

- Find five traditional stories or local legends from your school or local library. Make notes on openings (recording where you found the stories) and compare them. How do they gain the listener's attention and set the scene? Are there any common techniques which they use? Share your notes with your group to see if they have noticed similar patterns.

DETAILED DESCRIPTIONS

The following details (continued over the page) are taken from a version of *Sir Gawain and the Green Knight* told by Hugh Lupton of the Company of Storytellers...

'...there were whole roast oxen cooked in their gravy, there were whole roast sheep basted with honey, there were whole roast salmon splattered with butter. There were sweet things to suck, savoury things to crunch, sour things to savour and all washed down with a strong wine, mead...'

'...and this knight was green. His hair was green, his face was green, his great green beard spread across a green chest, green legs, green sandals on his feet and his horse was green from the tips of his ears to the hooves on his feet.

And in one hand the green knight was carrying a great green axe and in the other hand a bunch of holly bobbing with red berries. And the eyes in the green knight's head were as red as the holly berries...'

WORKING WITH DESCRIPTIONS

The first description is of a feast. Not only are we told what was eaten and drunk at the feast, we also know how things were cooked, what they were served with and how they tasted.

- Read this description aloud in different ways, using your voice to emphasise different things. Tape record each person's reading and decide which sounds most effective. This will give you an idea of how to use your voice to make the most of any detailed description.

- The second description is much more than just a description. Discuss the effects of the repetition with other members of your group.

- Choose a section from the story you are going to tell. Take it in turns to describe every detail in that section. Try to use a variety of ways to build up detail. Try including repetition for emphasis. Remember how Hugh Lupton uses all these techniques!

LANGUAGE

The story *Sir Gawain and the Green Knight* is a medieval tale, so the language that the storyteller uses will in many ways show this. The following extracts from the story show how Hugh Lupton does this:

'...and so it was...'

'...our honour is in your safe-keeping...'

'...strike steady cousin...'

'...the body of the green knight didn't falter or fail, it stayed steady...'

'...and he knew that to fail in the quest was to lose his honour...'

'...asking that he should find a place...'

'...and he was full of a strange warmth...'

'...and soon the great portcullis was lifted...'

'...welcome stranger...'

'...the lord of the castle, he threw back his head...'

'...the lord and his liegemen...'

SELECTING LANGUAGE

- Think back to your own chosen story. Make a list of words, phrases and sentence structures which are special to the time, people or places in your story.

- Practice reading a section of your story on to tape, without breaking the

atmosphere by using modern words or fillers like 'yeah' or 'right'. In your groups, listen to each others' tapes, and help each other to use the kind of language which fits the style of the story.

• Variety of language is important when telling a story, because it will help hold the attention of your listeners. Make a list of alternatives to the words in the columns below. (The first one has been done for you.) See if you can find more than one alternative, using a thesaurus to help you. Do the alternatives mean slightly different things from each other?

NOUNS	VERBS	ADJECTIVES
soup = broth	cry = weep	nice = pleasant
night =	speak =	bad =
female =	look =	large =
story =	move =	small =

• Rhymes and rhythms can be effective ways of emphasising ideas, or of making a story memorable. (Almost everyone remembers the queen's rhyme in 'Snow White and the Seven Dwarfs'.) You have already looked at rhythms created by repetition. However, 'Sir Gawain and the Green Knight' contains many places where the storyteller makes an idea memorable for the listener by using rhyme. For example:

'…whether fate be foul or fair

what can a man do but dare?…

• Go back to the story you've chosen for retelling. Note down any rhymes that are in the story, and write them down so that you can learn them. If there aren't any rhymes, it may be a good idea to invent at least one, and bring it in at an important part in the story. This will help you make your story memorable for your listeners.

DIFFERENT VOICES

As a storyteller, you are the narrator of the story and you must choose which narrative voice is the most appropriate. If you tell your story from your point of view (even if you are pretending to be someone else, such as one of the characters), you use 'I'. This is called **first person narrative**. For example, 'I went outside'. **Second person narrative** is not often used for storytelling – you would be telling the story from the point of view of your audience. For example, 'You go outside'. Perhaps the most popular form is **third person narrative**. For example, 'he went outside'.

HELP

First person narrative - told from the point of view of 'I'.
Second person narrative - told from the point of view of 'you'.
Third person narrative - told from the point of view of 'he, she, they.'

• Each kind of narrative voice creates a different effect. Read the sentences below and discuss the effects with your group. Think about the effect you want to create in your own story.

'I knew the creature couldn't see me, but I pressed still further back into the shadows.'
'You know the creature can't see you, but you press still further back into the shadows.'
'James knew the creature couldn't see him, but he pressed still further back into the shadows.'

WHICH VOICE?

The voice of the storyteller as narrator is important but so too are the voices the storyteller uses for the different characters in the story. Where possible a storyteller should try different tones, accents, **dialects**, paces, pitches and volumes.

• Think carefully about the story you have chosen. Discuss together appropriate places where you think different voices could be used in your retelling. Make a note of whatever you decide to do.

HELP

People from different parts of the country often speak different **dialects** – a person who speaks the same language as you may use different words or phrases, or may put words together in a different way. Look for the two examples of dialect among the endings which follow.

LAST LINES

The last lines of a story should provide an ending your listeners will enjoy.

'....As for the girl, some say she married, some say not. It matters little. What is certain is that she lived happily ever after.'

'And Jack had four wee laddies and two wee lassies, a happy family! But the happiest o' the whole life wi Jack was sittin roon the fire tellin the weans a story - how he'd cheated a ghost!'

From *Don't Look Back Jack! Scottish Traveller Tales* by Duncan Williamson

'So guess what Anansi did? Spin a web. He spun this web. Well, that was the first time he ever spun a web. He was so cornered. He just spins a web, quick, quick, quick right up to the ceiling so they couldn't catch him. But from that day until today, spider spinning web and living up in house-top and is Anansi make it.'

From 'Anansi and the Muzzirollinkinnah' by Louise Bennet in *That'd Be Telling*

'Three golden apples fell down from the sky, one for the storyteller, one for the listener and one for the one who heard.'

COLLECTING ENDINGS

- Begin to build yourself a collection of different types of endings. Look at examples from traditional tales and make up some of your own.

- Write another entry in your journal summarising what you feel you've learned about becoming a storyteller and what you still need to work at to improve.

HELP

These extracts come from pupils' journals and will give you some idea of the kinds of things to include in your own journal.

'.. .I still need to concentrate on using my voice and looking at the audience...'

' ...I want to make the voices just right for the story...'

'...I am going to concentrate on my confidence...'

'..I am going to concentrate on building my gestures (hand movements), looking at my audience and not letting my voice wobble..'

TELL IT!

You are now ready to tell your story. First of all, you must consider your audience:

Discuss with your teacher whether you should tell your story to a small group, a large group, or even a whole class.

Draw a plan of where you will ask your audience to sit, and decide where you will sit or stand – remember that each member of the group needs to be able to see your face, hear you clearly and see any objects or pictures you might use.

Secondly, make sure that you have ready anything you want to use in your telling of the story (you may want to show a picture or you may have found an object which you can use).

THE STORYTELLER

- Wait until your audience is settled and quiet, then begin your story. Remember to look at your audience all the time you are speaking – you need to do this to keep their concentration focused on the story – if you look out of the window, they will follow your gaze and you will lose their concentration. Make your voice, face and actions as interesting as you can – give life to your characters.

  When you come to the end of your story, keep looking at your audience for a moment or two while the ending sinks in – if you get up or laugh or cough straight after your last word, the spell will be broken and your audience will immediately put the story out of mind.

- After telling your story, write another entry in your journal reviewing your experience as a storyteller. What was it like? Were you successful? How might it have been better?

HELP

These extracts come from pupils' journals and will give you some idea of the kind of things to include in your own journal.

'..When I told the story... I think I spoke too fast, but I did remember what I wanted to say.'

' ...I'm not very good at telling stories. I rush them and don't take my time to explain detail very well. I get confused and get parts wrong. This makes it difficult for the people listening...'

'...We changed quite a lot of our story... so it was slightly different every time we told it...'

'...It might have sounded better if I had remembered to use the part when I said, "They walked and they walked and they walked, they walked for a day, they walked for a week, they walked for a month, they walked for a year, they walked for a year and a day".'

'...To make it more interesting I must remember to give the characters different accents and try to use dialect.'

STORIES WRITTEN

The following story is a written version of a Norwegian folk tale. It would probably have been told and re-told for many years before it was written down.

THE SQUIRE'S BRIDE

- Take it in turns to read this tale aloud. Listen carefully, because the ending is missing.

- Look out, also, for the way the storyteller uses the techniques that you've been studying.

THE SQUIRE'S BRIDE

An old Norwegian story

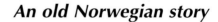

There was once a rich squire with a mint of silver in the barn and gold aplenty in the bank. He farmed over hill and dale, was ruddy and stout, yet he lacked a wife. So he had a mind to wed.

After all, since I am rich, he thought, I can pick and choose whatever maid I wish.

One afternoon the squire was wandering down the lane when he spotted a sturdy lass toiling in the hayfield. And he rubbed his grizzled chins, muttering to himself, 'Oh aye, I fancy she'd do all right, and save me a packet on wages too. Since she's poor and humble she'll take my offer, right enough'.

So he had her brought to the manor house where he sat her down, all hot and flustered.

'Now then, gal,' he began, 'I've a mind to take a wife'.

'Mind on then,' she said. 'One may mind of much and more.'

She wondered whether the old buffer had his sights set on her; why else should she be summoned?

'Aye, lass, I've picked thee out. Tha'll make a decent wife, sure enough.'

'No thank you,' said she, 'though much obliged, I'm sure'.

The squire's ruddy face turned ruby red; he was not used to people talking back. The more he blathered, the more she turned him down, and none too politely either. Yet the more she refused, the more he wanted what he could not have. With a final sigh, he dismissed the lass and sent for her father; perhaps the man would talk some sense into his daughter's head.

'Go to it, man,' the squire roared. 'I'll overlook the money you owe me and give you a meadow into the bargain. What d'ye say to that?'

'Oh, aye, Squire. Be sure I'll bring her round,' the father said. 'Pardon her plain speaking; she's young yet and don't know what's best.'

All the same, in spite of all his coaxing and bawling, the girl was adamant – she would not have the old miser even if he were made of gold! And that was that.

When the poor farmer did not return to the manor house with the girl's consent, the squire stormed and stamped impatiently. And next day he went to call on the man.

'Settle this matter right away,' he ranted on,

'or it'll be the worse for you. I won't bide a day longer for my bride'.

There was nothing for it. Together the master and the farmer hatched a plan: the squire was to see to all the wedding chores – parson, guests, wedding feast – and the farmer would send his daughter at the appointed hour. He would say nothing of the wedding to her, but just let her think that work awaited her up at the big house.

Of course, when she arrived she would be so dazzled by the wedding dress, afeared of the parson and awed by the guests that she would readily give her consent. How could a farm girl refuse the squire? And so it was arranged.

When all the guests had assembled at the manor and the white wedding gown laid out and the parson, in black hat and cloak, settled down, the master sent for a stable lad. 'Go to the farmer,' he ordered, 'and bring back what I'm promised. And be back here in two ticks or I'll tan your hide!'

The lad rushed off, wondering what the promise was. In no time at all he was knocking on the farmer's door.

'My master's sent me to fetch what you promised him,' panted the lad.

'Oh, aye, dare say he has,' the farmer said. 'She's down in the meadow; you'd better take her then.'

Off ran the lad to the meadow and found the daughter raking hay. 'I've come to fetch what your father promised the squire,' he said all out of breath.

It did not take long for the girl to figure out the plot.

So that's their game, she thought, a twinkle in her eye. 'Right, then, lad, you'd better take her then. It's the old grey mare grazing over there.'

With a leap and a bound the lad was on the grey mare's back and riding home at full gallop

Once there he leapt down at the door, dashed inside and called up to the squire,

'She's at the door now, Squire.'

'Well done,' called down the master. 'Take her up to my old mother's room.'

'But, master -'

'Don't but me, you scoundrel,' the old codger roared. 'If you can't manage her on your own, get someone else to help.'

On glimpsing the squire's angry face he knew it was no use arguing. So he called some farmhands and they set to work. Some pulled the old mare's ears, others pushed her rump; they heaved and shoved until finally they got her up the stairs and into the empty room. There they tied the reins to a bedpost and let her be.

Wiping the sweat from his brow, the lad now reported to the squire.

'That's the darndest job I've ever done,' he complained.

'Now send the wenches up to dress her in the wedding gown,' said the squire.

The stable lad stared.

'Get on with it, dung-head. And tell them not to forget the veil and crown. Jump to it!'

Forthwith the lad burst into the pantry to tell the news.

'Hey, listen here, go upstairs and dress the old mare in wedding clothes. That's what the master says. He must be playing a joke on his guests.'

The cooks and chambermaids all but split their sides with laughter. But in the end they scrambled up the stairs and dressed the poor grey mare as if she were a bride. That done, the lad went off once more to the squire.

'Right, lad, now bring her downstairs. I'll be in the drawing room with my guests. Just throw open the door and announce the bride.'

There came a noisy clatter and thumping on the stairs as the old grey mare was prodded down; at last she stood impatiently in the hallway before the door. Then, all at once, the door burst open and all the guests looked around in expectation.

WHICH ENDING AND WHY?

- The ending of this story has been left off. What ending do you think would work best? Talk about how the guests and the squire might have reacted in the final scene, what the girl might have done, and what the message of the story is. What clues has the storyteller given us already about these things? How does he want us to feel at this point? Why is that?

- Now write your ending in three paragraphs. Remember to use the storytelling techniques you have studied. Remember also to fit in with the way the storyteller has presented the characters, and the point that he is making. Finally, remember that an ending usually resolves all problems, although it doesn't always need to be a happy ending.

- In turn, read your ending to your group. Whose ending is best and why? Now read and discuss the real ending overleaf. List the ways it is similar to or different from your own endings. Can you explain why? How does this ending conclude the story effectively?

What a shock they got!

In trotted the old grey mare dressed up as a bride, with a crown sprawling on one ear, veil draped over her eyes, and gown covering her rump. Seeing the crowd, she let out a fierce neigh, turned tail and fled out of the house.

The parson spilled his glass of port all down his purple front; the squire gaped in amazement, the guests let out a roar of laughter that could be heard for miles around.

And the squire, they say, never went courting again.

As for the girl, some say she married, some say not. It matters little. What is certain is that she lived happily ever after.

From *The Woman in the Moon* by James Riordan

WRITING IT DOWN

Seeing a story written down is very different from hearing someone else tell it. Storytellers give their voices tone, pitch, pace and emphasis; they use gestures, actions and facial expressions. All these things help to bring their stories alive. An author, on the other hand, must help readers create or imagine these things for themselves.

LANGUAGE AND PUNCTUATION

- Look carefully over the story and find some examples of each of the following:

  1 someone speaking in dialect

  2 other words used instead of 'said'

  3 where the writer ends one stage of the action before leading into the next

  4 descriptions of the main characters

  5 some words or phrases which are not used much these days

- Write down what you find out, as all this detail will come in useful when you write your own story.

- Using your knowledge and what you've learned so far from this unit, make a list of as many things as possible that make a written story like this different from a story told. Draw a chart like the one below and add your group's ideas as you discuss these differences.

Comparing stories	
Spoken	Written
We hear the voices in the style they're meant to be.	*The writer describes how a character speaks.*

- List all the different punctuation marks you can find in this story, with one or two examples of each one. In pairs, write brief notes to remind you of the rules for using each of these punctuation marks. Then list reasons why punctuation is essential in a written story.

- In your journal, write about whether you would prefer to tell a story to an audience or to write a story. Make sure you give all your reasons why.

HELP

WRITING DOWN SPEECH

To show the actual words a speaker says, a writer uses speech marks:

" " or sometimes ' '

Look back at the story *The Squire's Bride* to find examples of speech marks being used to indicate where a person is actually speaking.

Points to note:

- The actual words spoken go inside the speech marks.
- Start a new line when someone else starts to speak.
- Put a dividing comma between the spoken part and the rest of the sentence.
- Put the dividing comma before the speech mark if the rest of the sentence comes next.
- There is no need for a dividing comma if there's an exclamation mark (!) or question mark (?).

For example:
"What do you want?" asked the King.
"I've heard your majesty likes to hear a good story," said Jack.
"I do, I do," replied the King.
"Well, I've come to tell you one," said Jack.
"Is it a good one?" asked the King, "If it isn't, I'll throw you in the deepest dungeon!"

WRITE IT!

As a final piece of work in this unit, you will write your own folk tale. You will plan your ideas in your group and then write a story on your own, using your group's plan. Follow the instructions below carefully. Once complete, your story will be one of many in a class anthology (collection of stories) which other students will enjoy reading.

WRITING YOUR OWN FOLK TALE

- In your group, brainstorm all the kinds of events, characters, objects and places which you would find in a traditional folk tale. Select from your list four objects, four characters, three places and two events which you would use in writing your own folk tale.

- Decide what kind of message your story might hold.

- Plan your folk tale.

  Think about:

  - the setting or situation

  - the problem

  - the actions, events and their results

  - the resolution

- Begin writing your own folk tale. You should **draft** the opening, following The Drafting Route on the opposite page. Remember what you have learned about the way traditional tales start.

  Think about:

  - introducing characters by their words and actions

  - setting up some kind of problem or dilemma to be sorted out

  - using an appropriate style to tell your story

- Try out your opening on a partner, then redraft it, improving the style, or adding to it. Then carry on with your story.

PUBLISH IT!

You might word process your story, and/or illustrate it before putting it into a class anthology.

THE DRAFTING ROUTE

When you have made notes on the subject and style of your project, and when you have made a list of useful words or phrases to help you write it, you can begin drafting:

PLAN

Make a rough plan of your piece of writing, including ideas about how you will begin, what will be your theme and how you will end the piece.

FIRST DRAFT

Write your first draft. Try to include all of the details you planned, keeping to the style in which you have chosen to write. Be careful with spelling and punctuation.

CHECK IT

Is it 'colourful' in description and does it contain enough details? How do you think it could be improved?

HAVE IT REVIEWED

Ask another member of your group to read your work and make constructive criticisms (review it), to help you see where you might improve it for your reader. Make sure you have a note of the points your friend makes.

FINAL DRAFT

Before you write your final draft, check any spellings you are unsure about in a dictionary, make sure that your punctuation is correct and gives the effects you want. Make any changes you need to, based on your reviewer's comments.

Write your final draft, making sure that your writing is clear. Your final draft may be illustrated and/or word processed. (Check that you have put your name on your piece of work.)

WHAT NEXT?

In this unit, you have developed your knowledge of stories and storytelling. You have also learned skills in oral and written storytelling. You may wish to build on these experiences by doing some further activities:

- Start a storytelling group in your class or school, but do not make the group too large. Agree to meet regularly to swap ideas and tell stories.

- Try to listen to as many storytellers in performance as possible. You may be able to ask them about their experiences as a storyteller.

- Talk to friends and relatives and ask them if they know any stories to tell you. Ask them if you can tape record them telling their stories. Your relatives will be able to remember stories from before you were born. You could write these down and make your own anthology.

'When we tell them, our stories are a tremendous gift'

Mary Medlicott

UNIT TWO

Personal Language File

In this unit you will concentrate on your own writing and reading skills and decide how you are going to improve them. You will develop your skills as:

SPEAKERS AND LISTENERS

by discussing your work with others
by talking about how you learn and what helps you learn most effectively

READERS

by looking at different styles of reading and practising the skills involved in them
by analysing and improving your own reading skills

WRITERS

by looking carefully at the areas you need to improve in your own writing
by producing your own Personal Language File that you can use as a reference guide to improve your writing.

This unit will equip you with the knowledge and skills that you need to produce a Personal Language File. Can you design, write and produce a file that will help you improve as a reader and writer? Turn the page to find out.

WHAT IS A PERSONAL LANGUAGE FILE

Your Personal Language File could be anything from a filofax to a diary with advice pages in it, or even a pop-up book. The look and feel of the final product will depend upon the decisions that you take as you work through the unit. You might decide simply to produce a file for your own personal use. You might get together as a class and decide to produce a single file which makes use of the best individual contributions, photocopying the finished product for everybody. You might even use the computer to produce a more polished version.

The first thing you need to do, however, is to become an expert. All writers make sure that they have fully researched their subject matter before they start writing. This unit is divided into three sections, covering the three things that you need to find out about before starting on the Personal Language File.

- Spelling awareness

- Making sense of sentences

- A good read

In each section, you will find the kind of information and ideas that you will need to produce your Personal Language File. From time to time you will come across a symbol that looks likes this. When this happens, it means that you need to make a decision about whether this is a topic that you might want to include in your File. If it is, the next step is to design and write a new page to be included in your Personal Language File. At the end of the unit is some further advice about how to make your pages as lively and interesting as you possibly can.

SPELLING AWARENESS

'IT DOESN'T LOOK RIGHT! WHAT IS GOING WRONG WITH MY SPELLING?'

Very often not all of the words you are trying to spell will be wrong. It is important to identify which part of the word doesn't look or sound right.
    Here is a selection of methods you could choose from.

WORD SHAPES

night

sight

right

WORDS WITHIN WORDS

There's a rat in separate

MNEMONICS

Big Elephants Can Always Use Some Eggs = BECAUSE

One collar, two sleeves = NECESSARY

RHYME

I'll be your friend

To the end

THE TEN MINUTE TEST

• Set yourself the ten minute test. Think of a subject that you can write plenty about e.g. family, pets, hobbies, school. Write constantly for ten minutes on your subject. When the ten minutes are up check for any errors in your spelling. List the words you need to learn and decide which method you will use to learn those spellings.

What works? Do you want to include any of these approaches in your Personal Language File? If so, design a really attractive advice page which will either remind you how to get your own spelling right or help somebody else.

'SPELLING RULES OK!'

You can help your spelling tremendously by paying attention to some of the spelling rules found in the English Language. Some are more common than others. Here is a selection for you to choose from. Do you know them or feel confident using them? Can you add to this list?

Adding 'ly' to adjectives

Ran quick-**ly**

Sang happi-**ly**

happy → happily

Split digraph

Vowel + consonant + **e**

rob
sam
cut   **e**
hop
rod

Changes sound of vowel from sound to name of it.

'i' before 'e' except after 'c'

rec**ei**ve	bel**ie**ve
rec**ei**pt	rel**ie**ve

'ff', 'll', 'ss' at the end of short words

fu**ll**
bu**ff**
stu**ff**
bo**ss**
fi**ll**

One 'l' at end of words with more than one syllable

beautifu**l**
wonderfu**l**

Doubling rule

Words where the vowel makes a long sound are often followed by a single consonant:
di**n**ing room, a**l**ways
Short vowels are followed by a double consonant:
fo**g**otten, impo**ss**ible

Drop 'e' before adding 'ing'

hope - **ing**   hoping
cope - **ing**   coping

Plurals

Most nouns add 's' to make more than one, - Bats
'es' - to words that end in 's', 'ss', 'x', 'sh', 'ch' - bo**x**es
'ies' replaces 'y'
ally   -   allies
copy   -   copies
hobby   -

Silent letters

'b'	com**b**
'h'	**h**onest
'g'	**g**nome
'k'	**k**now

• Do you want to include a page on spelling rules in your Personal Language File? If so, you will need to choose a selection of rules that you find particularly helpful and think of memorable ways to communicate them.

'THERE...THEIR — MISTAKES ARE EASILY MADE'

SPELLING
SECTION 1
AWARENES

Do you recognise any of these common mistakes as yours?

Their – belonging to them
There – over there
They're – they are

Off or of?
A bunch of flowers
Switch off

Were – past tense 'we are'
Where – indicates place
We're – we are

Our – belonging to us
Are – we are shopping

it's – it is
its – shows possession so no apostrophe
who's – who is
whose – shows possession:
Whose is this?

Watch that 'v'
knife ➡ knives
life ➡ lives

two – number 2
to – go to a place
too – too much

Add 'ly'
usual ➡ usually
hopeful ➡ hopefully
careful ➡ carefully
And 'oes'
potato ➡ potatoes
tomato ➡ tomatoes
But
piano ➡ pianos
photo ➡ photos

Word Pairs
here, hear
quite, quiet
weather, whether
altogether, all together
sight, site
accept, except
know, no
witch, which
peace, piece
through, threw
allowed, aloud
by, buy

• Look at your own work. What are your most common mistakes? List them in your workbook so that you can decide whether to include a section in your Personal Language File on commonly confused words.

KEEP IT IN THE FAMILY

Sometimes it helps to learn spellings if you can see the connections between similar words that are only different because something has been added at the beginning (a prefix) or at the end (a suffix).

Prefixes

Look at the prefixes listed below.

Prefix	meaning
Pre	before
Bi	two
Ex	out of
Mis	wrong
Re	back, again
Tri	three
Com	with
Em	in
Inter	between
Pro	for
Un	not

In addition to these prefixes, there are a number of prefixes which give the main word its opposite meaning as in de-frost, dis-like, un-kind, in-convenient.

Suffixes

Suffixes don't usually change the meaning of a word, but they do enable you to use it in a different way. Adjectives, for example, can often be turned into adverbs by adding 'ly' at the end. By adding 'ly', bright becomes 'brightly'.

- Choose five of the prefixes from the table and use a dictionary to see if you can find three words that have been created by adding that prefix.

- Sometimes when you add a suffix, the spelling of the word changes. Do some research to see if you can find any of the rules that apply when you add a suffix.

  Is 'Word Families' a section that you might want to include in your Personal Language File?

SPELL IT OUT – LEARNING TO SPELL

SPELLING SECTION 1 AWARENESS

If you have been working your way through the unit, you will have discovered that there are all sorts of different ways of learning to spell. To the right is a list of different approaches. Put them in rank order, starting with the one that you think would be most helpful, and finishing with the one that you think would be least helpful. Compare your list with a friend to find out if the differences tell you anything about how you learn most effectively.

Pinning lists to the bedroom
    ceiling, or the living room door

Playing Hangman

Doing crosswords

Playing Scrabble

Making tapes of difficult words and
    rehearsing them

Doing spelling quizzes

Playing 'My word'

Using a spellchecker on the computer

Inventing spelling rules

COMPARISONS

- Look at the extracts from three school text books on the following page, aimed at people of your age. First of all, think about the language features used by these texts, and tick the boxes in the chart below if you spot a feature. Then discuss which text is most helpful for a learner, and how these features contribute to that effect.

	English Today	All, Full and Till	Spelling 9 – 13
Pronoun to show speaker of text (*we*)			
Pronoun to show audience (*you*)			
Formal language			
Friendly language			
Imperative verbs			
Modal verbs			
Simple sentences (One clause only)			
Co-ordinate clauses (and/but/or)			
Subordinate clauses (other connectives)			

- You may want to return to this section for ideas for your Personal Language File. Use your comparison between the three extracts to make some notes on how best to give advice about learning spelling.

ENGLISH TODAY

SPELLING

The educated citizen must be able to spell correctly, for the simple reason that if we all spelt differently we should get into an appalling muddle. The best way to learn to spell is to notice the spelling of the more tricky words every time you meet them in print. There are, however, certain rules to help you with your spelling, and we shall from time to time give lists to show how these rules work.

From the following list draw up your own rule for the spelling of the EE sound (as in "meet") with "ie" or "ei":

believe	chieftain	shriek
thief	conceit	receive
ceiling	deceit	retriever
relief	receipt	retriever
siege	perceive	handkerchief
niece	fierce	weird } *exceptions*
		seize

Extract One

ALL, FULL AND TILL

When *all*, *full* and *till* are joined to a word or syllable, they drop an L:

a. all
- also
- always
- almost
- already
- altogether
- although
- almighty
- alright (*all* right *is better English*)

b. full
- hopeful
- grateful
- shameful
- joyful
- dreadful
- frightful
- helpful
- painful
- fulfil
- fulsome

c. till
- until

Extract Two

Extract Three

Dictation: He is always awful until all his tills are full.

SPELLING 9–13

HOW TO LEARN A SPELLING

Trying to spell a word you don't know

Sometimes we have to use common sense to have a go at spellings we don't know, making the best possible guess. Here's a way of having a go at a spelling:

Spell it bit by bit

Break the work down into syllables and spell them one at a time. This is a good method for long words such as:

manu-fact-ure (four syllables)

pop-u-la-tion (four syllables)

Say the following words out loud and count how many syllables they have:

dog

garden

poetry

education

MAKING SENSE OF SENTENCES

BREAK IT UP — WRITING IN SENTENCES

To convey meaning clearly when we write, we must use correctly-punctuated sentences. At school, you will lose marks if you don't write in complete, accurately-punctuated sentences when you are asked to do so. You should also know how to use a variety of sentence types and patterns, to suit your purpose and audience when writing.

Sidney Stringer Community Technology College Faculty of English

You need to know that there are different kinds of sentence-patterns:

A **simple sentence** has just one clause. *Claire went to the cinema.*

A **compound sentence** has two or more clauses joined by the **co-ordinating conjunctions** *and/or/but*. *Justin bought a coat* **but** *it was too small.*

And:

A **complex sentence** has a main clause joined to one or more subordinate clauses by **subordinating conjunctions** (all conjunctions apart from *and/or/but*), or by relative pronouns (*who, whose, which, what, that*). *While Sam was waiting, he read a magazine.*

HELP

CONJUNCTIONS

Compound and complex sentences often use conjunctions. Below is a list of the most commonly used conjunctions:

and	when	where
or	while	unless
but	before	until
so	after	because
although	whereas	if

SELF EVALUATION

Pick a page from a piece of writing which you have recently completed.

- Count up the number of simple sentences you have used.

- Now count up the number of compound sentences, the number of complex sentences, and the number of compound -complex sentences you have used.

- Do you use one pattern more than another, or are the patterns evenly balanced?

In your file, you should find an effective way of explaining the different patterns of sentences you can use. You should also include a section which sets targets for improving your use of sentences. You should first think about being accurate with simple and compound sentences, and then trying out a range of complex and complex-compound sentences. Set a target to widen the range of conjunctions that you use.

Dear Fred

The weather is hot.

The food is fantastic.

I wish you were here.

Love

Jane x

F. Smith

3 Church Road

England

? In pairs think of other examples of when short and long sentences are used. What differences are there

The ship is sinking fast
<STOP>

All hope is lost.
<STOP>

I may not survive
<STOP>

'I SAY, I SAY' — PUNCTUATING DIRECT SPEECH

When writing stories you may well want to include some dialogue.
Do you know the rules for using speech marks?

SELECTING LANGUAGE

- Look at the following sentences which show you how speech marks are used.

  "Run to the shops and get me some milk," said John.
  John said, "Run to the shops and get me some milk."
  "Run to the shops," said John, "and get me some milk."
  "Run to the shops and get me some milk," said John. "Two pints should be enough."
  "Do I have to ?" asked Sarah. "I'm tired."

- Complete these sentences on a separate sheet.

  1 You use speech marks to show…

  2 Speech marks are placed…

  3 The first word of direct speech always starts with…

  4 When someone new starts to speak you always…

  5 A comma is used to…

  6 This comma is always placed…

  7 The only reason you wouldn't use a comma for speech punctuation is…

'SAID IS DEAD'

- Sometimes the way in which writers report direct speech can become a bit repetitive – He said,… she said,… he said,… Challenge your partner to see who can find the most alternatives to the word 'said'. Here are some to start you off:

laughed, screamed, complained, grumbled, interrupted

- Now read the poem, *Teacher Said…*

Teacher said…

You can use
    mumbled and muttered,
    groaned, grumbled and uttered,
    professed, droned or stuttered
          … but *don't* use SAID!
You can use
    rant or recite,
    yell, yodel or snort,
    bellow, murmur or moan,
    you can grunt or just groan
          … but *don't* use SAID!
You can
    hum, howl and hail,
    scream, screech, shriek or bawl,
    squeak, snivel or squeal
    with a blood–curdling wail
          … but *don't* use SAID!
          … SAID my teacher.

- Look at your own story writing. Do you set out dialogue correctly? How many times have you used the word 'said'? Could you improve your writing by using an alternative? What steps will you need to take to improve your use of dialogue?

- It is hard to imagine a Personal Language File without a section on punctuating direct speech. How could you make your version really eye-catching and memorable?

MINIBREAKS: USING COMMAS

Look at the following passage from *Northern Lights*. Can you work out when and why the writer has used commas? List your reasons.

She looked fierce and stubborn as she sat there, small against the high carved back of the chair. The two old men couldn't help smiling, but whereas Farder Coram's smile was a hesitant, rich, complicated expression that trembled across his face like sunlight chasing shadows on a windy March day, John Faa's smile was slow, warm, plain and kindly.

"You better tell us what you did hear your uncle say that evening," said John Faa. "Don't leave anything out, mind. Tell us everything."

HELP

COMMAS

Single commas are used:

- to separate each item in a list of adjectives or nouns
- to mark off words or phrases that give extra information in a sentence
- to mark off dialogue in direct speech
- to separate clauses within a sentence

Commas are used in pairs:

- to mark off words, phrases or clauses giving extra information within a sentence (like brackets).

A comma can never join one sentence to another sentence.

If you decide to include a section on commas in your Personal Language File, you will need to provide a bit more information than in the Help Box on this page.

- How might you explain about commas to somebody who was finding it difficult to know when to use a comma and when to use a full stop?

- Write simple instructions about how to use commas, giving an example of each use.

'THAT'S A GOOD IDEA' – EXPLAINING COMPLICATED IDEAS

Sometimes you need to organise your writing so that it is more easily understood. To do this you could use:

Bullet points:

- Useful if there are several points to make.

- Easy to see on the page.

- Breaks up the text on the page.

A flow chart:

> Useful if information moves from one point to the next in sequence.

> Can be arranged across or down the page

Brackets or parentheses:

You can also arrange complicated information in sentences by using **brackets** or **parentheses** which mark off words which are not part of the main sentence.

For example try replacing the brackets with a pair of commas in the following sentence. How is the effect different?:

After waiting a long time at the bus stop (which is on Church Street) she caught a bus to the next village.

RESEARCH

- Can you think of any other ways to organise complicated ideas? How might you use grids and charts? What can you find out about 'mind maps', 'time lines' and 'spider diagrams'? Do you ever use sub-headings or information boxes?

- When you start writing your Personal Language File, you might decide to include some of these hints about organising complicated ideas in a section on making notes. If you do, you should make sure that you give clear guidance about which techniques to use in any particular situation. A flow diagram, for example, is not particularly helpful to explain a chronological sequence of events which might be better served by a 'time line'.

PARAGRAPHING

Read the article below about wolves.
The article has been printed without paragraphs.

Who's afraid of the Big Bad Wolf?

It's time to huff, puff and blow away the idea that wolves are bad. Yes, there were stories about how big bad wolves tried to eat a girl called Little Red Riding Hood and her grandmother and the Three Little Pigs. But those are just fairy tales. "Wolves are kind, gentle and caring animals by nature; they are also highly sensitive and highly intelligent," says Terri Smith, a breeder of wolf hybrids who hails from Virginia in America. Wolf hybrids are cross-breeds of dogs and wolves and Terri has raised a number since 1987. "If anyone tries to tell you that a wolf or a wolf hybrid is an evil, blood-thirsty animal, then tell them to come to my home and meet my precious hybrids," she continues. "Play with them, love and stroke them, and they'll respond with kindness. The most they will do is howl at you, but only as a greeting." Many people in early America would not have agreed with Terri. In those days, many settlers came to hate the wolves that killed their sheep and cattle, even though some were aware that the wolves were actually searching for food. To ensure the safety of their herds, the ranchers shot, poisoned and trapped all the wolves they could. As a result, as many as two million wolves were destroyed during the 1880's. In 1919, the US Government even hired hunters to remove all the wolves from their land. Americans were not the only people wary of wolves. Many Europeans viewed this animal as an evil and vicious creature. Some even believed that through the power of magic, men and women could change into werewolves at full moon periods. People who were suspected of being werewolves were burnt alive! Fortunately for wolves, people have now come to realise that they are not dangerous and wild killers. In America, the wolf is now classified as an endangered species.

PUTTING IN THE PARAGRAPHS

You are the editor of a magazine in which this article will appear.

- Copy and mark on the article where you think the paragraph breaks should go. Compare your decisions with a partner.

- Discuss with your partner why you made your decisions.

- Now between you produce a list of rules about using paragraphs.

- Compare your list of rules with those of another pair. Are there any you could add to your list?

Do you automatically set out your work in paragraphs? You need to decide whether your Personal Language File will include advice about paragraphs. If so, start by making sure that you have a record of all the rules that you have devised, whether working by yourself or with somebody else.

A GOOD READ

READ AT SPEED

A GOOD
SECTION **3** READ

It is not always necessary to read every word on a page to understand what the text is telling you or to get the information you need. If you are trying to get the main points of a piece of text it is probably best to **skim** the information.

Read the next bit of the article about wolves and decide on three key words that best sum up what you have read.

Those who would love to keep wolves as pets are allowed only wolf hybrids as it is against the law to own an endangered species.

The parents of wolf hybrids are often Alaskan malamute or huskie, as well as German Shepherd. These wolf-dogs have become very popular and it is said that there are half a million wolf hybrids living as domestic pets in the US today.

According to breeders, the ideal hybrid is family-oriented and sociable. It is also easy to handle and you can reason with it. The wolf hybrid understands many human emotions and is more intense with love and affection than any other animal.

"They feel more strongly towards humans than most dogs," says Terri. "Scientists have proven that wolves can think things out and make decisions, while dogs do things out of habit."

Once wolf hybrids are raised in a family, they can become depressed when forced to live alone. For them, being with a human is a thing that lasts forever.

"A wolf is an independent animal and it loves you until death. If you own any hybrids, make sure that your home and heart are open to them until they die," Terri advises.

So, young friends, the days of the Big Bad Wolf are over. Let the kind and gentle wolf into your mind and begin to love it.

If you are looking for a specific piece of information it is best to **scan** the text for the particular detail that you need. How would you read the article about wolves if you were just asked to find out how many wolf hybrids live as domestic pets in the US today?

These techniques are usually known as skimming and scanning. Do you want to include them in the Personal Language File? If so, how can you explain the difference?

SEARCHING FOR CLUES

A GOOD READ SECTION 3

Have a go at reading the following passages.

The most overwhelming difficulty experienced by the slow reader is that the decoding of print is _so_ laborious that comprehension of a passage is virtually impossible. The mechanical technique of reading creates a barrier to _understanding_. This exercise may help you to appreciate the problem. Your own comprehension of these sentences is probably severely threatened by your need to concentrate on the decoding problem which they present.

oe uo a ie ee a a eauiu ie o ie l e ae a oe l a ae a aa o ee. Eeo ou e a e uie ou eo l e o eaue e a o eauiu, aee a l. O, a ea ao e, e l! u l a o o a e a o a.

THS S TH STR F 'TH TMPST' PLY B WLLM SHKSPR. T S ST N N SLND N TH MDTRRNN. THS SLND S LRGL DSRTD BT NHBTD B TH SN F WTCH, CLLD CLBN. PRSPR, TH RGHTFL DK F MLN, ND HS DGHTR, MRND, HV BN MRND THR FR SM TM S RSLT F TH SFTHRTDNSS F N LD SRVNT. TN DK'S BRTHR, NTN, WTH TH HLP F TH KNG F NPLS, SCCDD N PLT T VRTHRW ND RPLC HS BRTHR S DK ND RDRD PRSPR ND HS DGHTR T B KLLD. TH PLY SHWS HW PRSPR, WH HS MGC PWRS, BGNS TO WK HS RVNG. T STRTS WTH STRM CRTD B PRSPR WTH TH HLP F HS SLV SPRT, RL. NTN ND LN S, KNG F NPLS, R SHPWRCKD WTH VRS F THR FLLWRS ND WSHB P N TH SHRS F THS SLND.

- • What is the subject of each passage?

  Not easy is it? What strategies did you use to try to decode the text?
- – Reading right to left?
- – Using patterns in words that are familiar?
- – Using your previous knowledge of the subject and the context?
- – Working out the vowels, beginning or ending of words?

- • Were there any others?

What do these puzzles tell you about reading? You might want to include a section in the Personal Language File which gives advice about what to do when reading becomes difficult because you don't have all the information you need.

INTO THE UNKNOWN

Everyone comes across words they cannot read straight away.
Here are some strategies you can use to help you decode words.

1 Reread the word in context to see if you can decide what the word is meant to be. Do the words around it help you to work out its meaning?

2 Break the word down into smaller components/syllables to see if there are smaller words that you can read in the larger word, e.g. com-part-ment, ex-plan-a-tion.

3 Having read the word correctly, it is important to understand its meaning. You may have been able to do this through reading it in context. If not, then using a dictionary or thesaurus is the best way to find the meaning.

UNFAMILIAR WORDS

The following extract contains a lot of unusual words – rare specimens that are not often sighted, even in books. It is taken from a book called *Captain Corelli's Mandolin* by Louis de Bernières. A doctor is about to remove with a fishhook a pea that has been stuck in a man's ear for many years …

This interjection gave the doctor pause; he reflected that if the pea was very hard, there was a good chance that the barb would not penetrate, but would drive the pea deeper into its recess. The drum might even be broken. He straightened up and twirled his white moustache reflectively with one forefinger. 'Change of plan,' he announced. 'I have decided upon further thought that it would be better to fill his ear with water and mollify the supererogatory occlusion. Kyria, you must keep this ear filled with warm water until I return this evening. Do not allow the patient to move, keep him lying on his side with his ear full. Is that understood?'

Dr Iannis returned at six o'clock and hooked the softened pea successfully without the aid of a hammer, small or otherwise. He worked it out deftly enough, and presented it to the couple for their inspection. Encrusted with thick dark wax, rank and malodorous, it was recognisable to neither of them as anything leguminous. 'It's very papilionaceous, is it not?' enquired the doctor.

Try the three stage technique described above to see if you can sort out what this extract is all about. How many of the words that you didn't know, could you correctly guess, and how many did you have to look up in a dictionary?

What advice would you give about the best way in which to tackle a difficult piece of writing, containing a lot of new words?

READING: THE WHOLE STORY

A GOOD
SECTION 3
READ

The message of this section has been that different kinds of writing needs to be read in different ways. Match the different styles of reading given below with the reading tasks shown in the cartoons.

scanning   skimming   decoding   close read   pleasure

READING STYLES

- How many situations can you think of when you need to use a particular reading style? Copy the table below and fill it in.

Situation	Reading Style

- Design an advert to promote one type of reading.
  Don't forget that it needs to be useful to you!

You may want to include ideas from this section for your Personal Language File. Use your survey of different types of reading to give advice about how to become good at making sense of a text.

DESIGNING YOUR PERSONAL LANGUAGE FILE

As you have worked through this unit you have started to develop some expertise about how language works. Now is your chance to build on that by completing and presenting your Personal Language File.

At each stage, you were invited to think about what you might want to include in the file. You now need to put it all together as a single document, deciding what goes in and what stays out. Start by drawing up a contents page, not forgetting to make space for extra material if there is anything that you can think of which has not been covered in the unit.

Following the decision about content, you need to

- design a front cover

- think of interesting ways of presenting the information you need. Why not create your own cartoon character or include pull-out or pop-up pages?

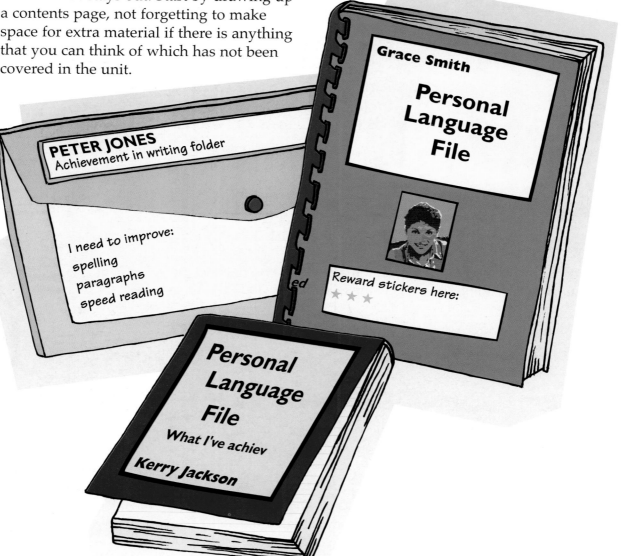

CREATING A TARGET PAGE

You will need to include a Target Page in your Personal Language File where you can list the particular weaknesses that you need to work on.

Think about the information you will need to include on your target page:

- Specific targets/rules

- How you will achieve your target

- Deadlines for review or reaching those targets

- Page numbers in your file which contain more information.

Design your page remembering to leave spaces to add other targets in the future. Don't forget to build in some rewards for yourself for when you reach those targets.

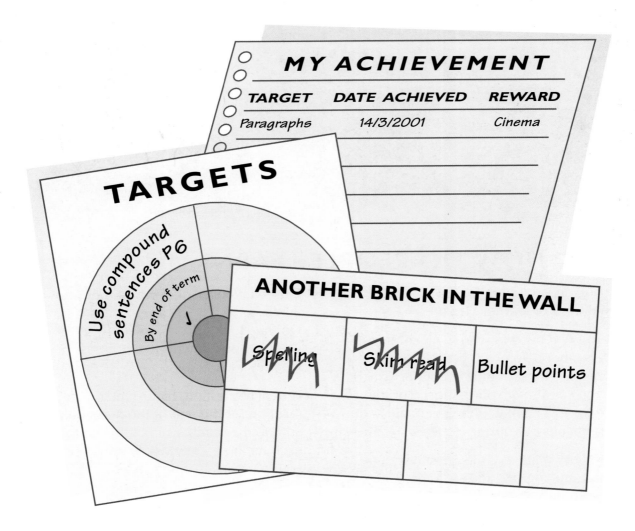

HOW DO WE LEARN?

Finally, there is one thing that you need to bear in mind when you are giving advice about how to improve your use of language. As learners, we all have different ways of making sure that we understand and can remember new ideas or information. The approach that you adopt is sometimes called your learning style. Think about something you learned recently. How did you do it?

More often than not people learn using more than one method. Their learning style will be a mixture of two or three methods but there may be a tendency for one method to be dominant. Learning styles can be categorised into 3 methods:

- Was it explained to you first?  • Auditory – by ear

- Did you read it in a book?  • Visual – by eye

- Was it demonstrated to you first and then you practised it • Kinaesthetic – by the senses

HOW DO PEOPLE LEARN?

This exercise will help you discover what kind of learner you are.

- You will need to work with somebody else, but before you get into pairs, prepare a list of quiz questions which you can fire at your partner. For this exercise, mental arithmetic works particularly well.

- In your pairs, ask the questions. Keep it fast-moving. The idea is to get your partner to answer quickly but to make sure they have to think hard as well.

- Observe your partner whilst they are thinking:
  Do they look up?
  Do they look down?
  Do they look across?

- For each question, record their reaction. At the end of the questioning add up the number of ticks given to each method. How would you describe your partner's learning style?

- Finally, repeat the process, swapping roles.

HOW DO YOU LEARN?

- Look at these statements. Tick them if they are true. Put a cross if they are not true for you. Leave them blank if you don't know.

Symbol	Statement	✔/✗
👂	I prefer things explained to me	
👂	I have a good memory and remember what people say	
✋	I like to have a go at things myself	
✋	I remember things better if I have a go myself	
👁	I like to be shown what to do	
👁	I remember what I have seen	
👁	I remember what I have read	
👂	I like to think about things first	
👁	I find it easier to follow diagrams rather than words	
👂	I find it easier to follow instructions rather than diagrams	
M	I prefer to work at my own pace and do not like to be rushed	
M	I like to work under pressure	
✋	I need to work things out for myself	
👂	I like to learn from others	
👂	I need to talk to others to see if I have the right idea	
M	It is easy for me to learn new things	
M	It is hard for me to learn new things	
M	I will only learn new things that I am interested in	
👂	It is easy for me to forget things unless I practise them	
👁	I find it easy to remember things when I have learned them	

- Using the symbols in the left-hand column, add up the number of statements you have ticked in each category. Are there more of one symbol than the others? If you have ticked any of the Ms this applies to how motivated you are and whether you need to do lots of relearning.

- Do your answers match what your partner said about you in the previous task?

WHAT NEXT?

In this unit you have looked at what makes writing effective and have analysed your own work in order to consider ways of improving your language skills.

You have produced your own Personal Language File where you have recorded information about language and have set targets for improvement. You should use this to help you with all your reading and writing.

To take this further you could:

- Look at other rules on spelling, punctuation and grammar (ask your teacher for books you could use). Consider which ones you need to learn and use and add them to your Personal Language file.

- Have a class book fair to display your Personal Language Files. Share ideas and add or rewrite pages for your own file.

- Revise your targets regularly throughout the year.

- Set up a 'Buddy' scheme where you help younger pupils or pupils in other classes to set their own language targets.

- Create a Personal File on Speaking and Listening. What skills do you need to improve and how could you do this?

The Mystery of the Lost Children

In this unit, you will look at different accounts of an event. You will gather evidence to write your own accounts in different styles. As you work through the unit you will develop your skills as:

SPEAKERS AND LISTENERS

by becoming journalists and detectives in order to solve a mystery
by looking for and talking about clues, and discussing what they might mean

READERS

by exploring the same story written as a poem and as a legend
by reading aloud in small groups and with the whole class
by collecting information to help you in your investigation

WRITERS

by writing in various styles that might be new to you, such as letters, newspaper articles, reports and leaflets
by telling your own story or legend

When you turn this page, you will see a picture of a stained glass window. It holds a number of clues about what happened in a small town in Germany many years ago.

In 1284 AD, 130 children disappeared from a small German town, the mystery has never been solved ...

26th June 1984

This plaque commemorates the loss, 700 years ago, of 130 children from this town.

THROUGH THE ARCHED WINDOW

- Look at the stained-glass window carefully. It provides glimpses of life in an ordinary town in 1284. What do you see? Make a list.

- The window provides all sorts of clues about what might have happened to the children who disappeared from the town. Draw up a second list of possible reasons for the children's disappearance.

The stained glass window	Reasons for the children's disappearance
A river	Floods in the town

- When you have completed your list, find out what everybody else in your group has done.

Yours very truly,
Robert Browning.

Like you, many people have speculated about this mystery. In the middle of the 19th Century, Robert Browning wrote a poem about it, which you may have heard or read. Find out what you can about Robert Browning's life, work and reputation. Then use the information to write a one-paragraph, 120-word entry on Browning for a new reference book to be called 'Great Writers of the Past: a young people's guide'. Aim to make the tone of your entry formal, but approachable for your audience.

THE PIED PIPER OF HAMELIN

by Robert Browning

I

Hamelin Town's in Brunswick,
By famous Hanover city;
The river Weser, deep and wide,
Washes its wall on the southern side;
A pleasanter spot you never spied
But, when begins my ditty,
Almost five hundred years ago,
To see the townsfolk suffer so
From vermin, was a pity.

II

Rats!
They fought the dogs, and killed the cats,
And bit the babies in the cradles,
And ate the cheeses out of the vats,
And licked the soup from the cooks' own ladles,
Split open the kegs of salted sprats,
Made nests inside men's Sunday hats,
And even spoiled the women's chats
By drowning their speaking
With shrieking and squeaking
In fifty different sharps and flats.

THE POEM

- Discuss which words you find puzzling and find out what they mean.

- Decide how to read the poem aloud. You could divide it up between you, using different voices for different parts.

- Prepare a reading of verse 2 that includes everybody in your class, even your teacher.

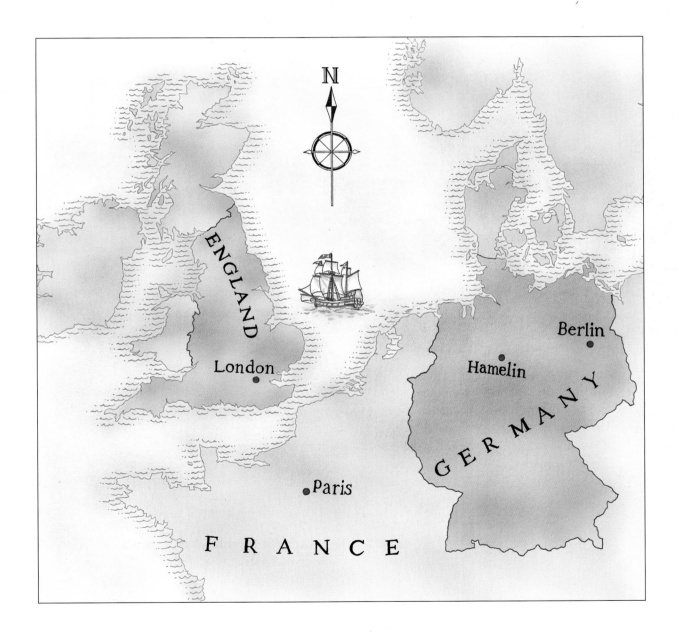

III

At last the people in a body
To the Town Hall came flocking:
'Tis clear,' they cried, 'our Mayor's a noddy;
And as for our Corporation – shocking
To think we buy gowns lined with ermine
For dolts that can't or won't determine
What's best to rid us of our vermin!

You hope, because you're old and obese,
To find in the furry civic robe ease?
Rouse up, Sirs! Give your brains a racking
To find the remedy we're lacking,
Or, sure as fate, we'll send you packing!'
At this the Mayor and Corporation
Quaked with a mighty consternation.

THE COUNCIL MEETING

- Working with a partner, imagine that you are one of the townspeople living in Hamelin in 1284. Talk about the problems that the rats are causing, and what people are doing about it.

> Those rats!
> They've been at the cheese again!

> That's nothing!
> One jumped on my baby's cradle!

- Still in pairs, take on the roles of the Major and the Corporation. As council members you have been elected to make sure that the town is run properly and you should be doing something about the rats, but it would cost a lot of money. What are you prepared to do?

> Hmm... there does seem to be a bit of a problem... people are rather upset!

> Perhaps we should do something about it... something not too expensive. What do you suggest?

- Hold a full meeting of the council in order to try to reach a decision about the problem of the rats.

  You need a volunteer to be the mayor and control the meeting. Somebody else should act as secretary and note down briefly what is said. These notes record what happened in the meeting and are called 'minutes'. They will be useful later.

Honourable members, the good citizens of Hamelin seem a little concerned about this rat business... you can probably hear the rabble at the door... What can we do?

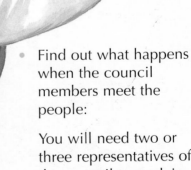

- Find out what happens when the council members meet the people:

  You will need two or three representatives of the council to explain the decision they have reached. In the roles of townspeople, the rest of the class should listen very carefully and then give their response. What would they say?

WHAT'S THE EVIDENCE?

If this poem by Browning is telling the true story, what kind of written evidence might there be to prove it?

- Look at the picture of the council's document chest. Can you think of any more documents that might be found in it years after the event?

- Decide which piece of evidence you are going to create and write it. Try to make your document look authentic (and old) and think hard about what sort of language would be appropriate. The tips provided on the opposite page will help you get it right.

GETTING RID OF RATS HANDY HINTS from HAMELIN HEALTH DEPT

PETITION To Mayor from Townspeople

TREASURER'S REPORT Council expenditure 1284

LETTER OF PROTEST

MINUTES OF MEETING

?

101 USES FOR A DEAD RAT

H.C.

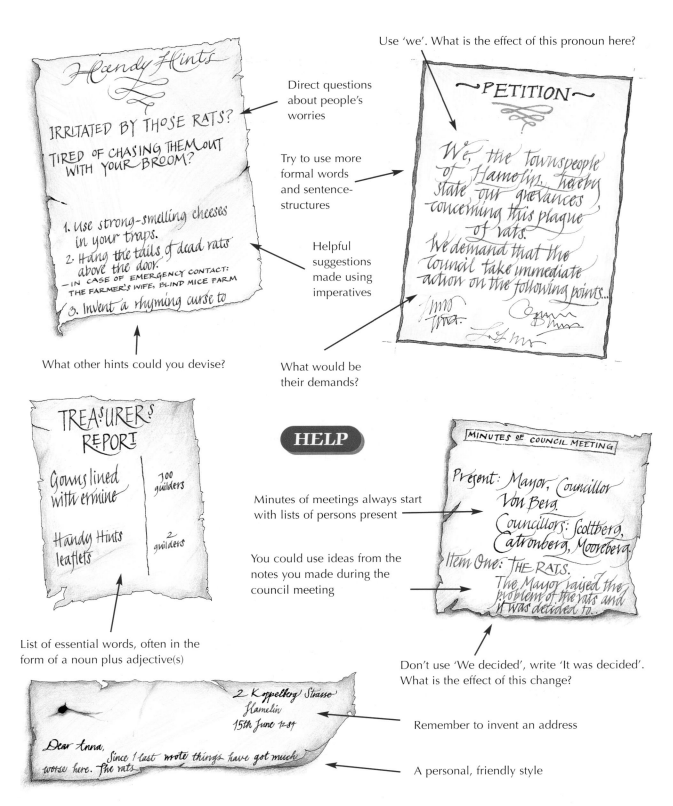

Use 'we'. What is the effect of this pronoun here?

Direct questions about people's worries

Try to use more formal words and sentence-structures

Helpful suggestions made using imperatives

Handy Hints

IRRITATED BY THOSE RATS?
TIRED OF CHASING THEM OUT WITH YOUR BROOM?

1. Use strong-smelling cheeses in your traps.
2. Hang the tails of dead rats above the door.
— IN CASE OF EMERGENCY CONTACT: THE FARMER'S WIFE, BLIND MICE FARM
3. Invent a rhyming curse to

What other hints could you devise?

~PETITION~

We, the townspeople of Hamelin, hereby state our grievances concerning this plague of rats.
We demand that the council take immediate action on the following points...

What would be their demands?

TREASURER'S REPORT

Gowns lined with ermine ... 700 guilders

Handy Hints leaflets ... 2 guilders

List of essential words, often in the form of a noun plus adjective(s)

HELP

Minutes of meetings always start with lists of persons present

You could use ideas from the notes you made during the council meeting

MINUTES OF COUNCIL MEETING

Present: Mayor, Councillor Von Berg.
Councillors: Scoltberg, Catronberg, Mooreberg.
Item One: THE RATS.
The Mayor raised the problem of the rats and it was decided to...

Don't use 'We decided', write 'It was decided'. What is the effect of this change?

Remember to invent an address

A personal, friendly style

2 Koppelberg Strasse
Hamelin
15th June 1284

Dear Anna,
Since I last wrote things have got much worse here. The rats

What other kinds of letters might there be in this document chest?
How might their style be different from these examples?

IV

An hour they sat in council,
At length the Mayor broke silence:
'For a guilder I'd my ermine gown sell;
I wish I were a mile hence!
It's easy to bid one rack one's brain –
I'm sure my poor head aches again
I've scratched it so, and all in vain.
Oh for a trap, a trap, a trap!'
Just as he said this, what should hap
At the chamber door but a gentle tap?
'Bless us,' cried the Mayor, 'what's that?
(With the Corporation as he sat,
Looking little though wondrous fat;
Nor brighter was his eye, nor moister
Than a too-long-opened oyster,
Save when at noon his paunch grew mutinous
For a plate of turtle green and glutinous)
'Only a scraping of shoes on the mat?
Anything like the sound of a rat
Makes my heart go pit-a-pat!'

V

'Come in!' – the Mayor cried, looking bigger:
And in did come the strangest figure!
His queer long coat from heel to head
Was half of yellow and half of red;
And he himself was tall and thin,
With sharp blue eyes, each like a pin,
And light loose hair, yet swarthy skin,
No tuft on cheek nor beard on chin,
But lips where smiles went out and in –
There was no guessing his kith and kin!
And nobody could enough admire
The tall man and his quaint attire:
Quoth one: 'It's as my great-grandsire,
Starting up at the Trump of Doom's tone,
Had walked this way from his painted tombstone!

VI

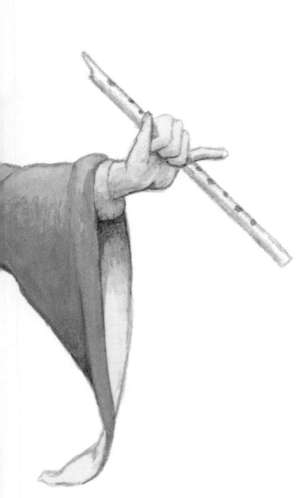

He advanced to the council-table:
And, 'Please your honours,' said he, 'I'm able,
By means of a secret charm to draw
All creatures living beneath the sun,
That creep or swim or fly or run,
After me so as you never saw!
And I chiefly use my charm
On creatures that do people harm,
The mole and toad and newt and viper:
And people call me the Pied Piper.'
(And here they noticed round his neck
A scarf of red and yellow stripe,
To match with his coat of the selfsame cheque;
And at the scarf's end hung a pipe;
And his fingers, they noticed, were ever straying
As if impatient to be playing
Upon this pipe, as low it dangled
Over his vesture so old-fangled.)
'Yet,' he said, he 'poor piper as I am,
In Tarty I freed the Cham,
Last June, from his huge swarms of gnats;
I eased in Asia the Nizam
Of a monstrous brood of vampyre-bats:
And as for what your brain bewilders,
If I can rid your town of rats
Will you give me a thousand guilders?'
'One? fifty thousand!' - was the exclamation
Of the astonished Mayor and Corporation

THE AGREEMENT

- The Pied Piper thinks that he has reached an agreement with the Mayor and the Corporation. It isn't clear whether a contract has been drawn up, but maybe it should have been. What do you think should be included in it?

- In groups of three, draw up the contract. Choose one person to be the Pied Piper and one to be the mayor. The third person should make notes to record what has been said.

- In your group of three, draw up and agree

> If I can rid your town of rats, will you give me a thousand guilders?

> Certainly! More perhaps! But only if you...

CONTRACT

I, the Mayor of Hamelin, in this year of 1284, agree to pay the sum of

VII

Into the street the Piper stepped,
Smiling first a little smile,
As if he knew what magic slept
In his quiet pipe the while;
Then, like a musical adept,
To blow the pipe his lips he wrinkled,
And green and blue his sharp eyes twinkled
Like a candle-flame where salt is sprinkled;
And ere three shrill notes the pipe uttered,
You heard as if an army muttered;
And the muttering grew to a grumbling;
And the grumbling grew to a mighty rumbling;
And out of the houses the rats came tumbling.
Great rats, small rats, lean rats, brawny rats,
Brown rats, black rats, grey rats, tawny rats,
Great rats, small rats, lean rats, brawny rats,
Brown rats, black rats, grey rats, tawny rats,

Grave old plodders, gay young friskers,
Fathers, mothers, uncles, cousins,
Cocking tails and pricking whiskers,
Families by ten and dozens,
Brothers, sisters, husbands, wives –
Followed the Piper for their lives.
From street to street he piped advancing.
And step for step they following dancing,
Until they came to the river Weser
Wherein all plunged and perished!
– Save one who, stout as Julius Caesar,
Swam across and lived to carry
(As he, the manuscript he cherished)
To Rat-land home his commentary:

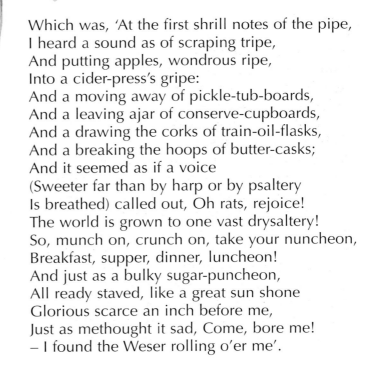

Which was, 'At the first shrill notes of the pipe,
I heard a sound as of scraping tripe,
And putting apples, wondrous ripe,
Into a cider-press's gripe:
And a moving away of pickle-tub-boards,
And a leaving ajar of conserve-cupboards,
And a drawing the corks of train-oil-flasks,
And a breaking the hoops of butter-casks;
And it seemed as if a voice
(Sweeter far than by harp or by psaltery
Is breathed) called out, Oh rats, rejoice!
The world is grown to one vast drysaltery!
So, munch on, crunch on, take your nuncheon,
Breakfast, supper, dinner, luncheon!
And just as a bulky sugar-puncheon,
All ready staved, like a great sun shone
Glorious scarce an inch before me,
Just as methought it sad, Come, bore me!
– I found the Weser rolling o'er me'.

VIII

You should have heard the Hamelin people
Ringing the bells till they rocked the steeple.
'Go,' cried the Mayor, 'and get long poles!
Poke out the nests and block up the holes!
Consult with carpenters and builders,
And leave in our town not even a trace
Of the rats!' – when suddenly, up the face
Of the Piper perked in the market-place,
With a, 'First, if you please, my thousand guilders!'

WHAT'S THE STORY?

- Working with a partner, conduct an interview with an eye-witness in order to find out exactly what happened. One of you will need to be the eye-witness, the other a reporter who has had a tip-off that something strange is going on in Hamelin...

    Before you start, make a list of the sort of questions that the reporter might ask, and read verse VII again very carefully, looking for answers.

    Think about how and where such an interview might be conducted and then put yourself in position for it. Would you stand or sit? How would you record the information you are given? Tape? Notebook? Begin when you are ready.

- When you have completed the first interview, swap roles and try again. Keep going until you are satisfied that you have got the whole story.

- Using the information from the interviews, write the front page article in that evening's edition of *The Hamelin Mail*.

Sub-heading

Headline

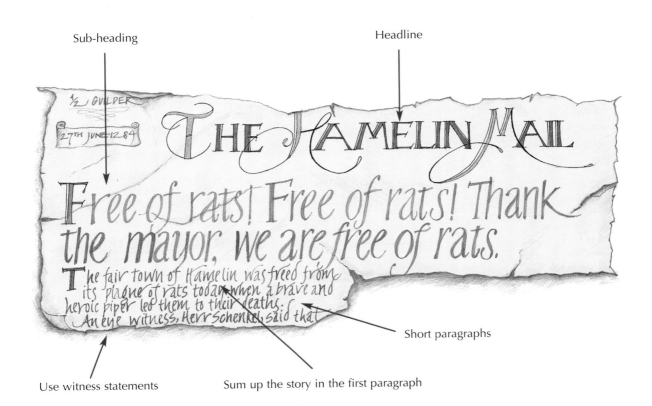

Short paragraphs

Use witness statements

Sum up the story in the first paragraph

A DIFFERENT POINT OF VIEW

In Ratland, things would have been viewed very differently...

½ guilder **Ratland Gazette** 27TH June 1284

Hamelin Horror: Thousands mysteriously drown in river tragedy

- Organise yourselves into groups of four, and re-read stanza VII, concentrating on the one rat who escaped. Why was he the only one who got away? Make notes on what he experienced when the Piper began to play, and what the rat would have seen when he and the others were being led to the River Weser.

- Now work out together, the story which the rat would tell on his return to Ratland. Use the notes you have made (although you can add more detail of your own), to get across the full horror of the rat's experiences. When you have finished and practised, one or more of you should tell the story to the rest of the class.

- This story will form the basis of the front page article in this evening's 'Ratland Gazette', which you are going to write. List all the details you will need to refer to. Think carefully about how the people of Hamelin and the rats would use different words to write about the same things. (Make a chart like the one below to help you.) Now write the article.

Rat-speak...		...Hamelin-speak
Cruel, vicious two-legged persecutors...	*The people of Hamelin*	Good, honest citizens...
Mass murderer	*The Pied Piper*	Our saviour: brave and heroic...

IX

A thousand guilders! The Mayor looked blue;
So did the Corporation too.
For council dinners made rare havoc
With Claret, Moselle, Vin-de-Grave, Hock;
And half the money would replenish
Their cellar's biggest butt with Rhenish.
To pay this sum to a wandering fellow
With a gipsy coat of red and yellow!
'Beside,' quoth the Mayor with a knowing wink,
'Our business was done at the river's brink;
We saw with our eyes the vermin sink,
And what's dead can't come to life, I think.
So, friend, we're not the folks to shrink
From the duty of giving you something for drink,
And a matter of money to put in your poke;
But as for the guilders, what we spoke
Of them, as you very well know, was in joke.
Besides, our losses have made us thrifty.
A thousand guilders! Come, take fifty!'

X

The Piper's face fell, and he cried,
'No trifling! I can't wait, beside!
I've promised to visit by dinner time
Bagdat, and accept the prime
Of the Head-Cook's pottage, all he's rich in,
For having left, in the Caliph's kitchen,
Of a nest of scorpions no survivor –
With him I proved no bargain-driver,
With you, don't think I'll bate a stiver!
And folks who put me in a passion
May find me pipe to another fashion.'

XI

'How?' cried the Mayor 'd'ye think I'll brook
Being worse treated than a Cook?
Insulted by a lazy ribald
With idle pipe and vesture piebald?
You threaten us, fellow? Do your worst,
Blow your pipe there till you burst!'

XII

Once more he stepped into the street;
And to his lips again
Laid his long pipe of smooth straight cane;
And ere he blew three notes (such sweet
Soft notes as yet musician's cunning
Never gave the enraptured air)
There was a rustling, that seemed like a bustling
Of merry crowds justling at pitching and hustling,
Small feet were pattering, wooden shoes clattering,
Little hands clapping and little tongues chattering,
And, like fowls in a farm-yard when barley is scattering.

Out came the children running.
All the little boys and girls,
With rosy cheeks and flaxen curls,
And sparkling eyes and teeth like pearls,
Tripping and skipping, ran merrily after
The wonderful music with shouting and laughter.

XIII

The Mayor was dumb, and the Council stood
As if they were changed into blocks of wood,
Unable to move a step, or cry
To the children merrily skipping by –
And could only follow with the eye
That joyous crowd at the Piper's back.
But how the Mayor was on the rack,
And the wretched Council's bosoms beat,
As the Piper turned from the High Street
To where the Weser rolled its waters
Right in the way of their sons and daughters!
However, he turned from South to West,
And to Koppelberg Hill his steps addressed,
And after him the children pressed;
Great was the joy in every breast.
'He never can cross that mighty top!
He's forced to let the piping drop,
And we shall see our children stop!'
When, lo, as they reached the mountain's side,
A wondrous portal opened wide,
As if a cavern was suddenly hollowed;
And the Piper advanced and the children followed,
And when all were in to the very last,
The door in the mountain-side shut fast.
Did I say, all? No! One was lame,
And could not dance the whole of the way;
And in after years, if you would blame
His sadness, he was used to say, –
'It's dull in our town since my playmates left!
I can't forget that I'm bereft
Of all the pleasant sights they see,
Which the Piper also promised me.
For he led us, he said, to a joyous land,
Joining the town and just at hand,
Where waters gushed and fruit-trees grew,
And flowers put forth a fairer hue,
And everything was bright and new;
The sparrows were brighter than peacocks here,
And their dogs outran our fallow deer,
And honey-bees had lost their stings.

And horses were born with eagles' wings:
And just as I became assured
My lame foot would be speedily cured,
The music stopped and I stood still,
And found myself outside the Hill,
Left alone against my will,
To go now limping as before,
And never hear of that country more!'

XIV

Alas, alas for Hamelin!
There came into many a burgher's pate
A text which says, that Heaven's Gate
Opes to the Rich at as easy rate
As the needle's eye takes a camel in!
The Mayor sent East, West, North and South,
To offer the Piper, by word of mouth,
Wherever it was men's lot to find him,
Silver and gold to his heart's content,
If he'd only return the way he went,
And bring the children behind him.
But when they saw 'twas a lost endeavour,
And Piper and dancers were gone for ever,
They made a decree that lawyers never
Should think their records dated duly
If, after the day of the month and year,
These words did not as well appear,
'And so long after what happened here
On the Twenty-second of July,
Thirteen hundred and seventy-six:'
And the better in memory to fix
The place of the children's last retreat,
They called it, the Pied Piper's Street-
Where anyone playing on the pipe or tabor
Was sure for the future to lose his labour.
Nor suffered they hostelry or tavern
To shock with mirth a street so solemn;
But opposite the place of the cavern
They wrote the story on a column,
And on the great Church-Window painted

The same, to make the world acquainted
How their children were stolen away;
And there it stands to this very day.
And I must not omit to say
That in Transylvania there's a tribe
Of alien people that ascribe
The outlandish ways and dress
On which their neighbours lay such stress,
To their fathers and mothers have risen
Out of some subterraneous prison
Into which they were trepanned
Long time ago in a mighty band
Out of Hamelin town in Brunswick land,
But how or why, they don't understand.

XV

So, Willy, let me and you be wipers
Of scores out with all men – especially pipers:
And, whether they pipe us free from rats or from mice,
If we've promised them aught, let us keep our promise.

You have now read one version of the events that took place in Hamelin all those years ago. Browning's ideas came from a legend, written down in the 19th Century by two brothers, Jacob and Wilhelm Grimm, who were collectors of folk-tales. Here is the version of the story which they wrote.

THE CHILDREN OF HAMELN

A wondrous man appeared in the town of Hameln in the year 1284. He wore a coat of many bright colours from which he is said to have acquired the name Pied Piper. He proclaimed himself a ratcatcher, and he promised to rid the city of all mice and rats in exchange for a certain sum. The citizens accepted his offer and promised him the requested amount of money as his reward.

The ratcatcher then drew out a small fife and began playing. The rats and mice immediately came creeping out of all the houses and gathered around him. When he was certain that none remained behind, he began marching out of town with the entire horde following after him. He led them down to the Weser River where he rolled up his clothes and marched right into the water, followed by all the creatures, who then drowned.

After the citizens had been delivered from this plague, they regretted having promised so much money. Using all kinds of excuses, they denied the man his reward, and he departed in bitterness and anger. Then, on the morning of June twenty-sixth, St. John's and St. Paul's Day – some say at seven o'clock, others say at noon – he reappeared as a hunter with a terrifying countenance, wearing a strange red hat.

Once again the sounds of his fife were heard in the streets and alleys. This time, however, instead of rats and mice came children. Boys and girls from four years of age on ran after him in great numbers, among them the grown daughter of the town mayor. The troupe of children followed him as he played, and he led them outside the town where they disappeared with him into a mountain.

A nurserymaid with a child in her arms, who had been approaching the town from afar and witnessed all this, brought the report to the city. The parents ran en masse to the gates, seeking their children with grieving hearts. All the mothers were weeping and wailing. Messengers were sent out in all directions by land, sea, and riverways to discover if anyone had seen or heard of the children – but all in vain.

Altogether, one hundred and thirty children were lost. Some people say that two of them returned some time later, but one was blind and the other dumb. The blind one could not point out the place but was able to tell how they had followed the Piper, and the dumb one could point out the place though he could tell nothing. One child joining the others was in his nightshirt and turned around to get his coat. He thus escaped the tragedy, for when he returned, the others had already disappeared into a cave in the hillside, which people still point out today.

The street on which the children marched out through the gate was still called – in the middle of the eighteenth century and probably still today – the Silent Street because no dance could be held and no musical instrument could be played there. Indeed, even when a bride was led to church in a procession, the musicians had to cross that street in complete silence.

The mountain near Hameln where the children disappeared is called Mt. Poppen. Two stone crosses have been erected to the right and to the left of the mountain. Some say the children were led into a cave and emerged again in Transylvania.

The citizens of Hameln recorded the event in their city register, and ever since have been in the habit of dating all their announcements from the day that their children were lost.

INVESTIGATING THE LEGEND

- Make a list of everything that is the same in the two versions of the story and one of everything that is different.

- Which version did you find most convincing, and why?

HELP

Having read two versions of the events surrounding the disappearance of the children of Hamelin, it is difficult to know what to believe. Some facts about life at that time are:

➡ children were sometimes kidnapped by rich landowners to work on their estates

➡ the crusades were taking place and Christians were travelling across Europe to fight the Muslims in the Holy Land. It was widely believed that innocent children were needed to help the Christian armies capture Jerusalem and so some 40,000 German children left to join the 'Children's Crusade'

➡ thousands of people died in the Black Death (the bubonic plague), a disease often carried by rats

EXPLANATIONS

- Look back at the stained glass window on pages 54 and 55 and remind yourself of the suggestions that you made to explain the disappearance of the children. What might have happened that led to the invention of the story of 'The Pied Piper'? Is there anything in the story itself that might provide a clue?

- Now write the text for a TV item to be called 'The Mystery of the Lost Children'. In this item you will briefly summarise the events in Hamelin all those years ago, and argue the case for your own explanation of what happened. You will need to look at the different versions of the story, at the range of evidence which exists, and at the way in which people's values and attitudes were different from today. The audience for the item will be the same age as you, or slightly younger.

a story book

a diary

a tape

a letter written by someone who knew the truth.

a cartoon

WHAT NEXT?

In this unit while you were investigating a mystery and discussing your findings, you were also developing your skills in speaking and listening. You have also read and produced for yourself written material in a variety of styles.

Having checked that you have completed all the tasks you need to from this unit, you may decide to go on to Unit 4. However, you may have completed Unit 3 sooner than you expected, in which case you could go on to do some of the following projects:

- Visit your school library or local library and find out all you can about rats – look at their habits and habitat. You could ask a local pet shop owner what he or she knows about rats and record his or her comments in a report about what you have learned. Illustrate your work with sketches or photographs. Write your report for inclusion in your school magazine, and argue that rats are misunderstood by most human beings.

- Find a newspaper article about an interesting or dramatic event. Write another version from the point of view of one of the people mentioned in the article. If there is a disagreement between people involved, you could take one role and find a partner who would take the other. Working together, discuss how differently each of you would regard the events, then write two contrasting versions of events, from your different viewpoints.

Quests and Journeys

Think about films you have seen, television programmes you watch, video games you play and books you have enjoyed. You may find that many of them involve people who go on quests or journeys to solve a mystery so that good triumphs over evil.

In this unit you will develop your skills as:

SPEAKERS AND LISTENERS

by becoming 'questers' and by solving puzzles and problems
by debating issues

READERS

by identifying the features of quest literature
by studying the language of different kinds of material

WRITERS

by writing a quest story of your own
by presenting information in different ways for different reasons

When you turn the page, you will start to read about quests and questers. You will be gathering information so that you are ready to become a quester yourself...

WHO GOES ON QUESTS?

Cam eyed the open sewer running down the middle of the street, reflecting the blue rag of sky among floating islands of the town's filth. There could be profit in sewers... Like the new one at Marseilles that dumped every turd in town on the Mayor's doorstep whenever it rained. It only needed deepening in one place and then worked perfectly. But it had taken Cam to spot that, and he'd walked away with three gold pieces. Cam lived off other men's stupidity. There was plenty of it about...

But the people of Marseilles had called him a young wizard. He hadn't liked that. The Church had a quick fiery end for wizards; and the man who accused the wizard got the three gold pieces... Cam left Marseilles quick; even left the Mayor's fine supper lying on his table.

He *wasn't* a wizard. He simply understood how the world fitted together; how axe joined handle, stream flowed from hill, rock broke wave.

Anyone could do that, who wasn't stupid.

From *The Cats of Seroster* by Robert Westall

...Bilbo sat down on a seat by his door, crossed his legs, and blew out a beautiful grey ring of smoke that sailed up into the air without breaking and floated away over The Hill.

'Very pretty!' said Gandalf. 'But I have no time to blow smoke-rings this morning. I am looking for someone to share in an adventure that I am arranging, and it's very difficult to find anyone.'

'I should think so – in these parts! We are plain quiet folk and I have no use for adventures. Nasty disturbing uncomfortable things! Make you late for dinner! I can't think what anyone sees in them,' said our Mr Baggins, and stuck one thumb behind his braces, and blew out another even bigger smoke-ring. Then he took out the morning letters, and began to read, pretending to take no more notice of the old man. He had decided he was not quite his sort, and wanted him to go away. But the old man did not move. He stood leaning on his stick and gazing at the hobbit without saying anything.

From *The Hobbit* by J.R.R. Tolkien

THE QUESTERS

Both of these characters will undertake great and dangerous quests.

- For each character, list the key details where the writers give us clues about what these characters are like. (Look at each character's actions and at what they say or think.)

- Compare the two characters. In what ways are they similar, and in what ways different?

- Which one would you expect to be more suited to a great and dangerous quest? What details show this?

- Can you predict (with reasons) how each writer will develop these characters in the rest of the story? Do the writers give us any clues?

- Start a journal to help you prepare for becoming a quester. In groups, list the kinds of characters who might go on quests and record your conclusions in your journal.

WITH A LITTLE HELP FROM YOUR FRIENDS

Often questers have helpful friends. Sometimes these friends come in surprising forms…

At about the same time – the distant church clock had already struck twelve – Momo was still sitting on the steps of the amphitheatre. She was waiting. For what, she didn't know, but some instinct had dissuaded her from going to bed.

All of a sudden, something light brushed against her bare foot. Peering hard, for it was very dark, she saw a big tortoise looking up at her. Its mouth seemed to curve in a mysterious smile, and there was such a friendly light in its shrewd, black eyes that Momo felt it was about to speak.

She bent down and tickled it under the chin. 'Who might you be?' she said softly. 'Nice of you to come and keep me company, Tortoise, even if nobody else will. What can I do for you?'

Momo wasn't sure whether she'd failed to notice them before, or whether they'd only just appeared, but she suddenly spotted some letters on the tortoise's back. They were faintly luminous and seemed to follow the natural patterns on its shell.

'FOLLOW ME,' she slowly deciphered.

Astonished, she sat up with a jerk. 'Do you mean me?' she asked.

But the tortoise had already set off. After a few steps it paused and looked back.

'It really does mean me!' Momo said to herself. She got up and went over to the creature. 'Keep going,' she told it softly, 'I'm right behind you.'

And step by step she followed the tortoise as it slowly, very slowly, led her out of the amphitheatre and headed for the city.

From *Momo* by Michael Ende

THE HELPERS

- What clues has the writer given us about the possible strengths and weaknesses of Momo's new helper?

- What other 'helpers' can you think of who assist people on quests you have read about or seen?

- When your group has thought of some helpers, consider whether the helpers have some weaknesses as well as strengths, and why it would probably not be a good idea if a helper could solve all problems.

- Write down what you have discovered about helpers in your journal and make a note of the characteristics you might want in a helper if you were going on a quest.

WHY GO ON QUESTS?

Look carefully at these short outlines of six quest books from which you will find extracts in this unit.

Cats of Seroster
Cam's quest is to find the city's great golden cats and restore both them and the son of the murdered Duke to their rightful place. Little Paul, the evil leader of the rebels, stands in his path.

The Hobbit
Bilbo Baggins becomes the fourteenth member of the group assembled by the wizard Gandalf, to recover the treasure stolen from their ancestors by the dragon Smaug.

Momo
Momo, an orphan girl, embarks on a quest to free her city from the 'men in grey', time-thieves who are draining the life of her fellow citizens.

Enchanters' End Game
Garion, once a farm hand, discovers he is a descendant of Riva Iron-grip, once Overlord of the West. His quest is to recover the Orb of Aldur, and, as Overlord himself, restore peace to the land. His enemy is the God Torak.

The Neverending Story
Bastian is twelve, fat and frightened of school, not usually the stuff of heroes. But Bastian's imagination spirits him into the world of magic, where he is called upon to save a world falling into decay.

The Odyssey
Ulysses is successful in defeating his enemies and in destroying the city of Troy, but offends the God Poseidon by killing his son Cyclops, a one-eyed giant. Ulysses struggles to return to his home of Ithaca, but Poseidon, God of the Sea, constantly puts barriers in his path. The Goddess Athene is his friend.

A TEST OF CHARACTER

In most quest stories the quester faces a series of tests...

When Bilbo opened his eyes, he wondered if he had; for it was just as dark as with them shut. No one was anywhere near him. Just imagine his fright! He could hear nothing, see nothing and he could feel nothing except the stone of the floor.

Very slowly he got up and groped about on all fours, till he touched the wall of the tunnel; but neither up nor down it could he find anything: nothing at all, no sign of goblins, no sign of dwarves. His head was swimming, and he was far from certain even of the direction they had been going in when he had his fall. He guessed as well as he could, and crawled along for a good way...

He could not think what to do; nor could he think what had happened; or why he had been left behind; or why, if he had been left behind, the goblins had not caught him; or even why his head was sore...

But in slapping all his pockets and feeling all around himself for matches his hand came on the hilt of his little sword - the little dagger that he had got from the trolls, and that he had quite forgotten; nor fortunately had the goblins noticed it, as he wore it inside his breeches.

Now he drew it out. It shone pale and dim before his eyes. 'So it is an elvish blade, too,' he thought, 'and goblins are not very near, and yet not far enough.'

But somehow he was comforted. It was rather splendid to be wearing a blade made in Gondolin for the goblin-wars of which so many songs had been sung; and also he had noticed that such weapons made a great impression on goblins that came upon them suddenly.

'Go back?' he thought. 'No good at all! Go sideways? Impossible! Go forward? Only thing to do! On we go!'

From *The Hobbit* by J.R.R. Tolkien

FEATURES OF QUESTS

- Discuss in your group any similarities you can see in the reasons for the quests outlined on page 85 being undertaken. What other reasons might questers have to go on their quests? Do they all have something in common?

- Remember to make a note of your findings in your journal and write down what you think might be the most important reasons for going on a quest.

- Think about how Bilbo is being tested in the extract above. Do you think he passes the test?

- Can you think of other 'heroes' who are reluctant to commit themselves, but later change their minds? Discuss this with your group and see how many you can find.

- Why do you think it is important that these tests take place?

- Make a short entry in your journal on what you have learned about tests of character.

THE JOURNEY

A quest is not a quest without a journey...

Ire, hunger and thirst pursued Atreyu. It was two days since he had left the Swamps of Sadness, and since then he had been wandering through an empty rocky wilderness. What little provisions he had taken with him had sunk beneath the black waters with Artax. In vain, Atreyu dug his fingers into the clefts between stones in the hope of finding some little root, but nothing more grew there, not even moss or lichen.

At first, he was glad to feel solid ground beneath his feet, but little by little it came to him that he was worse off than ever. He was lost. He didn't even know what direction he was going in, for the dusky grayness was the same all around him. A cold wind blew over the needlelike rocks that rose up on all sides, blew and blew.

Uphill and uphill he plodded, but all he saw was distant mountains with still more distant ranges behind them, and so on to the horizon on all sides. And nothing living, not a beetle, not an ant, not even vultures which ordinarily follow the weary traveller until he falls by the wayside.

Doubt was no longer possible. This was the Land of the Dead Mountains. Few had seen them, and fewer still escaped from them alive...

The Neverending Story by Michael Ende

MAKING THE JOURNEY

- Discuss why journeys in quests are always difficult.

- What do these journeys add to the story, and what do they tell us about the character of those making the journey?

THE LAST, BIG BATTLE

In nearly all quests there is one last, big battle. In *Enchanters' End Game*, Garion, known as the Rivan King, comes face to face with Torak, the child of dark. Cthrek Goru is Torak's sword....

With an animal howl of anguish and rage, The Child of Dark raised Cthrek Goru above his head and ran at the Rivan King. Garion made no attempt to ward off the blow, but gripped the hilt of his flaming sword in both hands and, extending his blade before him, he lunged at the charging enemy.

It was so easy. The sword of the Rivan King slid into Torak's chest like a stick into water, and as it ran into the God's stiffening body, the power of the Orb surged up the flaring blade.

Torak's vast hand opened convulsively, and Cthrek Goru tumbled harmlessly from his grip. He opened his mouth to cry out, and blue flame gushed like blood from his mouth. He clawed at his face, ripping away the polished steel mask to reveal the hideously maimed features that had lain beneath. Tears started from his eyes, both the eye that was and that was not, but the tears were also fire, for the sword of the Rivan King buried in his chest filled him with its flame.

He lurched backward. With a steely slither, the sword slid out of his body. But the fire the blade had ignited within him did not go out. He clutched at the gaping wound, and blue flame spurted out between his fingers, spattering in little burning pools among the rotting stones about him.

His maimed face, still streaked with fiery tears, contorted in agony. He lifted that burning face to the heaving sky and raised his vast arms. In mortal anguish, the stricken God cried to heaven, "Mother!" and the sound of his voice echoed from the farthest star.

He stood so for a frozen moment, his arms upraised in supplication, and then he tottered and fell dead at Garion's feet.

Enchanters' End Game by David Eddings

BATTLE FOR POWER

The fight between Garion and Torak is the climax of the book.

- Look carefully at the language used. Is this just a fight between two powerful warriors or is it something more?

- List the words or phrases that suggest:

- the evil of Torak

- the good of Garion

- the importance of the fight

- Write in your journal what you have found to be important about the quester's journey and final battle.

HOMECOMING

When the quest is finally over there is usually a homecoming when the quester returns to the comfort and peace of home. After many years and adventures, Ulysses returns home to the island of Ithaca, where his wife Penelope does not accept that he really is her husband.

'I have heard it said that my cousin Helen was tricked in exactly the same way, when Paris put on the appearance of her husband Menelaus,' said Penelope.

Ulysses spoke to his son Telemachus. 'Son, your mother speaks wisely; for we have ways of knowing one another, secret from everyone else.'

Then Ulysses was bathed and dressed in beautiful clothes. Penelope felt almost sure this was her husband but still she had doubts. So, as a test, she said:

'Noble sir, let us wait until tomorrow until we test one another again. I will give orders to the maids to bring out the bed of Ulysses - the bed of Penelope and Ulysses, whom you claim to be.'

Then Ulysses was angry. He turned on her, saying, 'Who has been interfering with my bed? No-one, however strong, can lift that bed and bring it out. And I will tell you why: when I married you, and built on our bedchamber to the palace, there was an olive tree as thick as a pillar. Round this olive tree I built the room, and roofed it over. I cut off the lower branches and used the tree, which was still growing, as one of the corner posts of the bed. Lady, here is proof of who I am. I say that the bed cannot be brought out to me, unless some man has cut away the stem of the olive tree.'

When she heard this, Penelope's last doubt was gone. She then broke into weeping, and ran up to him, threw her arms about his neck and kissed him.

'Ulysses, my husband,' she said. 'None but you and I knew of the olive tree that is part of the bed in our secret bridal chamber. Now I know who you are, and I am truly happy once more!'

Then Ulysses held her in his arms; and in the happiness of that moment, it seemed that all his toils and wanderings were but little things compared with so true and great a joy.

From *The Odyssey* by Homer

FINAL TRIUMPH

- Discuss in your group why this ending suits this particular quest story.

- Think of the ending to another quest story you know. How is it different from or similar to this one? Why might that be?

- Discuss with your group – or think over yourself – what coming home from a long journey would mean to you. Why would it be important?

- Now write in your journal about the reason quest stories often end with a return home. What are the writers trying to show?

THE 'QUEST' GENRE

You have looked at seven extracts, all highlighting typical ingredients of the **genre** of quest stories. Now look at the grid opposite. Each ingredient is listed down the left hand side of the grid. One column has already been filled in, based on the film *Indiana Jones and the Temple of Doom*.

HELP

A **genre** is a 'type' of writing that conforms to certain rules and styles, and has certain features of language. You may have already looked at the genre of the folk tale, for example.

FINDING A PATTERN

- Draw your own grid and fill it in with the stages of two more quests: one film and one book.

  Follow the pattern of the Indiana Jones example on the opposite page.

THE PATTERN OF QUESTS

	Indiana Jones and the Temple of Doom	Another film	Another book
The Quester - (Who?)	Indiana Jones - a professor of archaelogy. Resourceful but scared of snakes. Skilful at using a whip which gets him out of difficult situations. Stumbles into quest by chance crash in Himalayas.		
The Quest - (Why?)	To find the Sankara stone stolen by an evil leader of a mysterious cult who has also taken and enslaved hundreds of children.		
Helpers - (Who?)	'Shorty' Round - a secret urchin from Shanghai, who is also resourceful, can drive a car - fights his own personal battle against the young Maharajah who is under the spell of the evil Thugee leader. Also, Willy Scott, a nightclub singer from Shanghai who reluctantly finds herself on the quest.		
The Journey - (Where?)	A plane journey from Shanghai across China takes Indiana, Willy Scott and Shorty to a Village high in the Himalayas. Hearing of the village's plight they travel to Pankot palace on Elephants, then on foot to recover the missing Sankara stone.		
Trials and Tests - (How?)	In Pankot palace's secret passageways. The spike room. In the underground shrine to Kali - the cage that is lowered into the volcanic pit. In the mine workings on the rock crushing conveyor belt - and escaping the pursuers and the water in the mine in a cart.		
The Final Challenge - (The climax)	On the rope bridge and on the sheer cliff face. Indiana and the evil High Priest of Thugee duel in a final battle.		
Homecoming - (Afterwards)	Indiana returns to the Indian village with the stone and the children bringing happiness. Indiana and Willy Scott get together despite both pretending they did not like each other. Indiana gives up a fortune by not taking the valuable stone back with him but has no regrets.		

YOUR ADVENTURE

- Following the instructions on the next few pages, you will be able to write your own quest story. Keep in mind the points you thought of when you discussed the reasons for a quest and what the quester learns on his/her journey. You can refer back to your journal to refresh your memory. Discuss with your teacher whether you should work as a group or on your own.

- First of all, read the cartoon on pages 92–93 and write a neat summary of the problem you need to solve.

CHAPTER 1 – THE TIME CAPSULE

➤ Describe how you discover the capsule and how you crack the code.

➤ Describe the discussions with your parents, and how you decide which two helpers to take.

➤ Draw a map of Great Britain as you think it might look in over 300 years time. Mark where you live. Make that spot the location of the dome. Draw a desert around where you live.

Find the place where the seeds are stored. Work out your route from where you live to the seeds, making sure you have to cross at least one river and one mountain range. You can, if you wish, draw in a river and mountain range that exist today, or you can make up your own. When you have drawn your map, give all the features place names. You could also colour your map.

Include any other dangers connected with pollution that you can think of. You could, for instance, have lakes of sulphuric acid. Think of weather conditions you might include.

Give your map a key to identify the hazards.

Note: A causeway now runs between Northern Ireland and Scotland. This is the result of an underwater volcanic explosion.

PROVISIONS

You are allowed to take the following:

- sand buggy

- acid rain resistant tent

- silver hats to protect against the dangerous rays from the sun

- a month's food and water

- oxygen tablets that will allow you to breathe

Decide what else you will need to take with you. You can take only six of the following, or the sand buggy will be overloaded:

- salt tablets

- unbreakable rope

- acid-resistant waders

- night sight binoculars

- sun block cream

- torch with two mile beam

- compass

- pocket computer giving up-to-the-minute weather conditions

- radar watches showing any form of life within a two mile radius

- thought projector, that enables you to ask advice from people at home.

Discuss in a group what you would take and what you would leave behind. Have clear reasons for your decisions.

Write about what you are taking and why you decided as you did.

CHAPTER 2 – THE DANGEROUS DESERT

Now you face your first major test – crossing the desert that surrounds the dome in which you live.

The dangers include:

- quicksand

- hot spots, where the ozone layer has been damaged and harmful rays reach the earth's surface

- roaming bands of thieves who have adapted to life without oxygen

- sudden sandstorms that can shift huge dunes on top of you

- areas where toxic waste has seeped up from underground

- acid rain storms

You may add to this list of dangers.

Write your second chapter of your quest. Describe your journey and mark your route on your map. Include at least three of the dangers. Explain how you overcome them. Remember the strengths and weaknesses of your helpers.

CHAPTER 3 – TRAPPED IN THE CITADEL

Having crossed the desert, you have fallen into the clutches of the oxygen thieves. The oxygen thieves live in the Citadel in Dark Mountain, from where they raid passers-by for their life-giving air. There a city has been built, protected from the dangers on the surface. The thieves decide to throw you into prison while they demand a ransom from the dome dwellers for your release. You can mark the Citadel on your map.

Luckily for you your jailer is a kind old man, who decides to give you a chance to escape. The trouble is that there are four routes to safety through the heart of the mountain. All have their own dangers. Bearing in mind the strengths and weaknesses of your chosen helpers, you must decide which path you will take.

On the cross-section of Dark Mountain are some of the dangers that you will meet. Using your wits and whatever you salvaged of your belongings, you make your escape. You overcome the dangers, but only just...

THE DANGERS

The Magma Hole. A drop of a hundred feet into red hot molten rock. There is no bridge...

The Corridor of Knives. A corridor one hundred metres long where knives spring out without warning at all heights.

The Nest of the Acid Ants. A towering nest of ants. Their bites paralyse.

The Thought Dragon. You must pass it without letting it read your thoughts. If it sees itself in your mind, you're history.

Too Hot to Handle. You must swing on rungs over a thousand foot drop. But the rungs get red hot, without warning...

The Deadly Spider. You must cross a giant cobweb. Tread too hard and the giant spider will awake.

The Flowers of Stone. Their perfume is so beautiful, you just have to smell ... and are turned to stone.

Snake Pass. The snake asks you riddles. Answer right, or you're snake meat...

✦ Write about your capture by the oxygen thieves, your escape with the help of the jailer, and how you overcome the dangers of Dark Mountain.

CHAPTER 4 – SURVIVING THE WATERFALL

Having escaped from the Citadel, you have continued your quest. You have travelled many days and are close to your destination. The next part of your journey is by river. You find a boat and make good progress. But now you come to the Falls of Doubt – a terrible waterfall and churning rapids that will crush you to a pulp... if you lose faith.

There is only one way to survive The Falls... by remembering why you have come on this quest, and your hopes for the future. If you can shout your beliefs above the roar of the spray, you may survive. So think carefully. Why have you risked your life on this perilous quest? What beliefs and hopes have kept you going so far?

✦ Describe the experience of going over the falls. Remember to describe not only what happens, but your feelings as you plunge through space. Include the beliefs and hopes you shout out, remembering to use speech marks.

CHAPTER 5 – THE LAST BATTLE

The end of the journey is in sight. Ahead lies the mountain, which you must approach by one of three valleys. Each valley is guarded by a monster which must be overcome. Each monster has ferocious powers, but also has one weak point. Remember the helpers and tools you have brought.

Grogan

An octopus-like monster with five tentacles that constantly sweep the valley floor in search of food. Each tentacle can curl round and crush the victim. Its one weak spot is a gap in the armour-like plating that covers its head. The gap is above the right eye.

Megatroth

A winged beast that paralyses victims with its poisonous spit. Its x-ray vision can detect movement for half a mile in front. The valley is half a mile wide. The megatroth's one weakness is beneath the chin, where its poison is stored.

Spiderene

A spider-like monster that lives in a cave, in the side of the mountain, it has woven 'superglue webs' that snare anyone who enters the valley. Its weaknesses are weak eyesight and a hatred of bright light.

You are weak after a long journey, but you still have your helpers. Review the strengths and weaknesses of your helpers. Decide which monster you would stand the most chance against.

✦ Describe the battle.

 # CHAPTER 6 – RECOVERING THE SEEDS

At last you have arrived at the final barrier – a secret door behind which the seeds are stored. But Professor Ericson took care, long ago, that it would not be easy to get in. The door is made of extremely thick steel, with a combination lock. To open the door, two words must be entered into the lock by turning the dial to the correct letters, in the right order. The first word is four letters, the second six letters.

The Professor has provided a clue in her notebooks – she has copied one of her favourite poems, 'To See the Rabbit'. The poem is about a future world where mankind has completely lost contact with the natural world. The rabbit in the title of the poem is the only rabbit left alive in the world, and the people of the future find it such a weird and wonderful creature that they travel miles just to get a look at it. The rabbit, not surprisingly, isn't so keen on the humans.

Ten words have been left out of the poem. Professor Ericson has included the missing words in the list printed after the poem. To find the words that will open the door, you must:

• Read the poem carefully, then work out the words from the list that fit the gaps. Do not rush. Working out the meaning of the poem, and the pattern in which words fall is the way to do it – guessing will just get you confused. If you are not sure of an answer go back to it later.

• The number from one to ten in each space refers to the letter in the word you have chosen. For instance, if you had put 'rabbit' in the space marked ❺ you would know that letter 5 of rabbit ('i') is one of the ten letters you are looking for to find the password for the steel door.

• When you have found all ten letters, rearrange them into a well known phrase or saying. Remember, the first word is four letters, the second is six letters.

✦ Describe what you found at the spot where the seeds are and what you have done to open the steel door. When you have discovered the password, describe how you open the door and what you find inside – remember that this should be a moment of triumph!

TO SEE THE RABBIT

We are going to see the rabbit.
We are going to see the rabbit.
Which rabbit, people say?
Which rabbit ask the children?
Which rabbit?
The only rabbit,
The only rabbit in England.
Sitting behind a barbed wire fence
Under the floodlights, neon lights,
Sodium lights,
Nibbling grass
On the only patch of grass
In England, in England
(except the ———❺——— by the hoardings
Which doesn't count).
We are going to see the rabbit
And we must be there on time.

First we shall go by escalator,
Then we shall go by ———❿———,
And then we shall go by ———❹———,
And then by helicopterway,
And the last ten yards we shall have to go
On foot.

And now we are going
All the way to see the rabbit,
We are nearly there,
We are longing to see it,
And so is the crowd
Which is here in ———❾———
With mounted policemen
And big loudspeakers
And bands and banners,
And ———❽——— has come a long way.
But soon we shall see it
Sitting and nibbling
The blades of grass
In – but something has gone wrong!
Why is everyone so angry,
Why is everyone jostling
And slanging and ———❸———?

The rabbit has gone,
Yes, the rabbit has gone.
He has actually ————**7**———— down into the earth
And made himself a warren, under the earth,
Despite all these people.
And what shall we do?
What can we do?

It is a pity, you must be ————**5**————,
Go home and do something else for today,
Go home again, go home for today.
For you cannot hear the rabbit, under the earth,
Remarking rather ————**2**———— to himself, by himself,
As he rests in his warren, under the earth:
'It won't be long, they are bound to come,
They are bound to come and find me, ————**1**———— here.'

Alan Brownjohn

Missing words

even	motorway
burrowed	disappointed
everyone	sadly
grass	underground
thousands	complaining

 # CHAPTER 7 – HOME FREE

You have found the secret seeds. After many adventures, you have returned home to the dome. You have a selection of seeds and can guide the dome dwellers to the rest.

— Describe the scene as you return, and your feelings as you greet your family and friends. Remember that this is the end of a long, hard journey. There should be a strong feeling of relief and happiness – as there was in the extract from *The Odyssey*.

— Will you ever be quite the same person you were when you set off? So much has happened. Describe your feelings as you reflect on the events of your quest.

If you have followed all the steps, you will now have written your own quest. Collect all you have written on the quest and keep it in a folder because you may go on to make it into a book at the end of this unit (page 104).

WHAT NEXT?

In this unit, you have read different pieces of quest literature and investigated common features. You have developed your skills as a writer by constructing your own quest.

You may find that you want to take one of these topics further:

- Make your quest into a book. First design your cover: take a piece of plain paper and turn it so that the longer edges are at the top and bottom. Divide it in half (by folding it, if you like) down the middle. Draw your front cover on the right hand side, not forgetting the title and author, and write a summary of what the book is about on the left hand side (the back cover). Gather together two more pieces of plain paper behind your cover and fold the pile down the middle. Write up your quest in neat on the inside pages, using one page per chapter, and illustrate the pages as you go along.

  Discuss with your teacher how to stick or staple the pages together when you have finished.

- In one sense, we still make quests when we travel to distant places. Companies that sell holidays remind us how exciting it is to travel to different places. Collect travel brochures and study the language. How do they describe holiday destinations to make them sound attractive? What would they be like if they told the whole truth? Try writing a glowing entry for a travel brochure about your home town, and then try one telling the truth.

- Saving the world is no job for one person. Every day, people are working to keep the world a safe, peaceful and healthy place. Invent a situation in which the environment is under threat for good reasons, for example a plan to build a convenient road which will divert traffic away from a local school but will cut through parkland, or to build a factory which brings jobs into the area but may cause some air pollution or noise. Draw a map to show a 'before' and 'after' plan of your chosen area. Include some important things that will be lost or damaged by the development. Also build in some benefits.

  Present a formal debate to the rest of the class, one person arguing for the development and another person arguing against. Prepare for this by listing the benefits and threats posed by the development. Think in advance what the other person might say: how are you going to answer their points? Can you find any evidence to back up your feelings? How will you introduce your points to get the listeners behind you? Try out your speech on a friend (or tape yourself) before you do your live speech. After the debate, ask the class to vote for or against the development.

ANSWERS

- Riddle (page 93) – BEN NEVIS
- To See The Rabbit (page 102) – OPEN SESAME

UNIT FIVE

The Snake-stone

In this unit you will investigate the plot, themes and characters of Berlie Doherty's novel *The Snake-stone*. You will develop your skills as:

SPEAKERS AND LISTENERS

by using drama activities to explore the novel
by working with others to understand some of the themes of the novel
by experimenting with informal and formal methods of speaking

READERS

by making plot and character notes on the novel
by studying characters, thinking about their ideas and what motivates them
by searching for an understanding of the other issues involved

WRITERS

by creating a folder of writing
by writing in a variety of formats and styles
by writing for an audience, requiring you to be accurate and clear, and to
    adopt the right tone

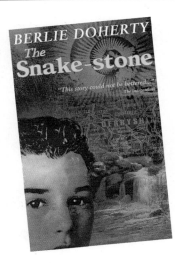

When you turn the page you will take a trip down memory lane. You will look at events in your own childhood and compare them to those of James – the main character in the novel *The Snake-Stone*. Think about the different kinds of up-bringing you and your classmates have had…

WHO AM I?

How far back does your memory go? Can you remember your first day at Primary School? Can you remember your fourth birthday? Can you remember a younger brother or sister being born? What is the very earliest memory that you have? Complete the following task before reading chapter 1.

- Think about the questions above for a while, then note down all you remember about your earliest memory. Now tell a partner about this memory, and why you think you have managed to remember it for so long.

- What do you know about your own birth? Use your memory to complete the following table on a separate sheet. What you can't remember, find out by asking people at home.

Place of birth	
Time & date of birth	
Birth weight & height	
Age of mother at that time	
Age of my father at that time	
Ages of brother/sisters at that time	
Where I first lived	

- What about photographs? Bring into school a small collection of photographs of your earliest days. (Perhaps you have pictures of yourself with your parents or relatives in the hospital; or being taken home; or as an infant lying down or crawling around the floor at home.) You might wish to organise a 'Guess the Baby' competition! Try to persuade your teacher to bring in some photographs too!

IMPORTANT KEEPSAKES AND MEMENTOES

Read Chapter 1 before completing the following tasks.

If you had to choose five keepsakes or mementoes of your own to take with you on a long journey away from home, what would they be? Write down a list of all the possibilities, then pick out the most important five. Write a brief explanation of why each is important to you. You could use a table like the one below.

Keepsake/Memento:	Why it is important to me:
1	
2	
3	
4	
5	

'I have a stone that looks like a snake: all curled up. It's my most precious thing. I've had it since I was born, you see.'

'I went up to my room and took out the letter that my diving coach in London had sent me last year. That was my most precious thing at the time.'

WHO IS HE?

NOTE-MAKING TO TRACK A *CHARACTER*

As you discover more about James you will need to make notes of your findings. You can break down your notes into:

(1) facts (what can be proved) – "*it **says it** in the text*"

(2) inferences and deductions (like 'reading between the lines')
– "***I can work it out*** from the text"

[continued over…]

Here's an example for you, using information from Chapter 1:

Facts	Inferences/deductions
• James was adopted	• He feels apart from his classmates

'This is not a fact, it is my opinion. It is what I have deduced (or inferred) from the following quotations.'

"Just this once I wanted to be one of them…"

"The other lads in the class never knocked about with me anyway."

Using a table is a good way to make notes in order to track a character through a novel. Draw up your own table for the character of James as he develops in *The Snake-stone*. Keep the following points in mind:

- Aim to write at least one point per column from each chapter that James writes.

- At certain points you will need to exchange ideas with others in your class. This will help you develop your thinking about the novel.

- Make notes in the same way for Elizabeth and James' mum and dad.

NOTE-MAKING TO TRACK THE *PLOT*

A useful way to keep track of a story or plot is to record the main events in a **flow chart**.

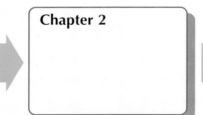

Chapter 1

James becomes interested in his birth

Elizabeth has baby.

Chapter 2

Sometimes more than one box may be necessary for an individual chapter. Or you could write Elizabeth's story in a different way to James' story, for example by using a different colour as above.

This kind of note-making will also help you:

- to locate important parts of the story quickly, for example if you are discussing or writing about it once you have finished reading;

- to write a summary of the story, because you will by then have written down the story's most important parts.

Start your own flow chart by copying the one above and adding some more key events for Chapter 1. Continue to add to your flow chart as you read.

Read from 'So on Thursdays Dad would pick Matt up...'
(three-quarters of the way through Chapter 3) to the end
of Chapter 4 before completing the following tasks.

1. Write a **factual report** of what happened in these pages. A factual report, or factual account, is the kind of thing a police officer might write at the scene of a crime. The intention is to record **only the facts** and no opinions, inferences or deductions. For example, have a look at the following. Which statements do you think are factual and which are giving opinions?

(a) *She was being very rude to the man.*

(b) *She was facing the man and speaking to him in a raised voice.*

(c) *He was dressed in a blue, floor-length coat.*

(d) *He was dressed in a strange coat.*

Break down your report into organised paragraphs. Aim to write between 100 and 150 words.

2. Discuss with a partner how you think James felt about

(a) the sport of diving

(b) his parents

(c) Matt's accident.

Make sure that you can support your opinions with evidence from the text. You might use some of your findings to put into your character notes.

3. Can you think of a time when you felt very angry with your own parents for something which you felt was their fault. What happened? Looking back on the incident, do you still feel that it was all their fault?

In small groups, choose an incident which would cause a child to feel angry with his/her parents. Act out this incident to the class in such a way as to show that there was, in fact, some fault on both the child's and the parent's sides.

1. Now read Chapter 5. Look at the description of Elizabeth taking the baby up on to the Tor.

Had to take it right away from home.

Someone would see me if I went to the village or down the lane to the main road. Someone would see me and tell Father. He would kill me if he knew.

I turned my back against the house, where the little ones were sleeping warm in their beds and Father was snoring.

I knew I had to take the skinny thing over the mountain tor.

Big, massy shape in the dark.

Never been up there, right to the top and over the other side.

They say planes crashed up there in the war, and the pilots were never found, and it's haunted by them.

They say boggarts climb out of the peat to lure you into the marshes.

The wind was full of sleet and squall. The little thing started to whimper, like a cat.

Pulled my coat tight round it. Went past Uncle Staff's lambing sheds with Bob scampering round my knees. No one about. Too early yet. Too early for the birds to start shouting.

I was too sore to climb over the stile. Had to put bundle down in the mud while I opened the gate.

Bob snuffled his face into it and I yanked him back.

Picked it up and shoved it back inside my coat. Felt it moving itself around.

Wondered if it would die before I got over the tor.

Wanted to find somewhere safe for it.

Didn't want it to die.

You are going to draw a map of the route she took, filling in all the geographical details of the scene. Update the map as you read on through the story.

- Begin by closely reading the lines written by Elizabeth and listing all the features which you could include on your map, for example:

  village – lane – main road – house

- You could also draw pictures of three key moments in this scene. Some of the features, for example the dog and the weather, could only be included in a picture, not a map. See if you can capture Elizabeth's emotions as she makes this terrible journey.

- This task may give you more details for your character note-making. Are you also remembering to keep your plot notes up to date?

2. The shock of Matt's accident leads to some changes in James' normal behaviour in Chapter 5, as well (to a lesser extent) to the behaviour of his mum and dad. Make a list of the changes that you notice. See if you can find at least five. Here are two to get you started:

(i) James realises that he *can* find his birth mother if he wants to

(ii) James doesn't want to swim

[*cont...*]

3. **Hot seating:** This task can be done as a whole class, with three pupils volunteering to take on the three character roles, or in groups of at least three, with each pupil taking on a role. Each of the three pupils takes on the roles of James, his mum and his dad. The remainder of the group, or class, will devise questions to find out how each character feels about Matt's accident, and how it has affected their own relationships at this point.

- If you are playing one of the three characters you will need to read the text carefully to understand his or her feelings at this time, and to help you to stay in role. If you are devising questions you too must read the text carefully to find challenging questions to ask the characters.

DIVING

Now read Chapter 7. What do you learn about the sport of diving in this chapter? Have a close look in particular at the early section of the chapter (from *"Coach would have written 'You must get plenty of sleep…'"* to *"It's about difficulty and style."*)

- Write down your findings about diving as a set of instructions for success in the sport. Here's a start for you:

1 Make sure you get plenty of sleep beforehand

2 Try to improve your maths otherwise it's hard to know how well you are scoring until the end

Aim to come up with at least five points of your own.

- Have you been diving yourself? Have you ever dived from the ten metre board or done anything else like this which could be dangerous? If you have, tell your classmates what it was like. Were your feelings similar to James' when he did it for the first time? Why did **you** do it?

CHALLENGES AND ACHIEVEMENTS

A dictionary definition of the noun '*challenge*' includes:

> an invitation to take part in a trial or contest … a test of one's abilities … a demanding or difficult task …

In Chapter 7 James explains how he became interested in and challenged by diving. Have you had any similar experiences? Have you set yourself any big challenges which you have then succeeded (or not succeeded!) in taking on? What do you hope to achieve this year, or before you leave school?

- What is your greatest achievement? Make a list of between three and five achievements of which you feel proud. Copy and complete this table:

Achievement	Why I feel proud of this
1	This makes me feel proud because…
2	I feel proud about this because…
3	
4	
5	

Of these I feel my greatest achievement is… because…

- Check the notes in your table through carefully. Choose **one** of your five achievements and **either**

  – write one paragraph (maximum 300 words) in which you

  a) describe what you achieved

  b) explain how you felt achieving it

  or

  – write a citation as if it had been written about you by somebody else, describing your achievement and why it was so impressive (maximum 300 words).

- Ask yourself the following questions:

  1. Have you explained your feelings **clearly** and **fully** giving plenty of **examples** when possible?

  2. Have you thought about sentence-structure, paragraphs and formality?

  3. Are your **spelling** and **punctuation** accurate?

HELP

A citation is a note which accompanies an award, describing the reasons for it.

LANGUAGE STUDY

Now read Chapter 9. Notice how Berlie Doherty uses animal imagery in this chapter. James compares his own behaviour to that of wild animals:

'*wily as a <u>fox</u>*' and '*my heart was prancing about like a <u>wildcat</u>.*'

When describing the behaviour of the woman in the ticket office he says:

'*She <u>tortoised</u> her head out of a yawn.*'

He compares Ken Eldred's wife to a bird:

'*She looks after Ken's divers like a chirpy <u>sparrow</u>,*' and '*she twittered*'

'*I hung up on her warbling*'

• Find these examples. What is the purpose of each description? What aspect of the character's behaviour is Berlie Doherty drawing your attention to in each case? It might help if you consider how the descriptions *could* have been written. For example, instead of comparing Ken's wife to a bird, Berlie Doherty could have written:

'*She looks after Ken's divers well*' and '*she said*' and '*I hung up on her talking*'.

How would the effect of this have been different?

• Using comparisons in this way is a useful technique which *you* could use in your own story-writing. What animal qualities do *you* have?! Think of the way you walk/run/dance, talk/shout/whisper, eat/drink, sleep/get up, etc. Could you use animal imagery to describe the way you do any of these things?

• What about someone else in your family? Use animal imagery to describe the way they do some of these things.

Action	Animal imagery
• walk/run	• I prowl like a hungry tiger
	• Mike waddles through the crowd
	• My sisters stampede through the house
	• My mum barked out instructions
	• Dad bounced in like a kangaroo

PRESENTATION: THE STORY SO FAR...

Read the end of Chapter 10. You have now read nearly half the book. This would be a useful point to stop and see what you have learnt about James and Elizabeth, and to make sure you have grasped what is going on in the story. You can do this by looking at your notes and comparing them to someone else's.

In your character notes you should have a good number of **facts** and **inferences** or **deductions** about James and Elizabeth. See p107 for definitions of inference and deduction if you need to remind yourself.

- In small groups, compare your findings. The facts should be clear, but you may well disagree on the inferences and deductions, because these are your opinions. Try, in each group, to come up with a group view of how James' or Elizabeth's character has developed during the novel so far.

- Each group should prepare a brief presentation to the class in which you will describe your group's view on what kind of a person James or Elizabeth is, based on the evidence in the book. Make sure that each person in the group has a part in the presentation. Look at the help box below for some guidance on delivering a presentation.

- When you feel ready, practice your presentation to your group or at home. Treat this as your 'first draft', just as you would a piece of writing.

You might want to try one of these two methods:

1. Each person in the group describes one key incident in James' or Elizabeth's story so far. Clearly describe what happened, then clearly explain what this tells you about his or her personality.

2. Each person in the group picks one adjective (or descriptive phrase) which describes James or Elizabeth, then gives one or two quotations from the text to support this adjective (or descriptive phrase). Refer to p107 on how to make inference/deduction notes for an example. Here Berlie Doherty is suggesting that James felt apart from his friends. You inferred this from the quotations that you wrote down as your evidence. So the quotations support the description.

HELP

RULES FOR MAKING AN EFFECTIVE PRESENTATION

- <u>Preparation</u> is very important. If possible, speak from notes rather than reading out your writing.

- Think about your <u>body language</u>: make eye contact with your audience and stand straight and strong! You may wish to emphasise points with hand gestures.

- Think about your <u>voice:</u> speak clearly, fluently and with appropriate pace and volume.

INSIDE A CHARACTER'S MIND

Now read Chapters 11 and 12. James' determination is put to the test here. He nearly gives up.

• What events occur which upset or disappoint him?

• What makes him decide to continue nonetheless?

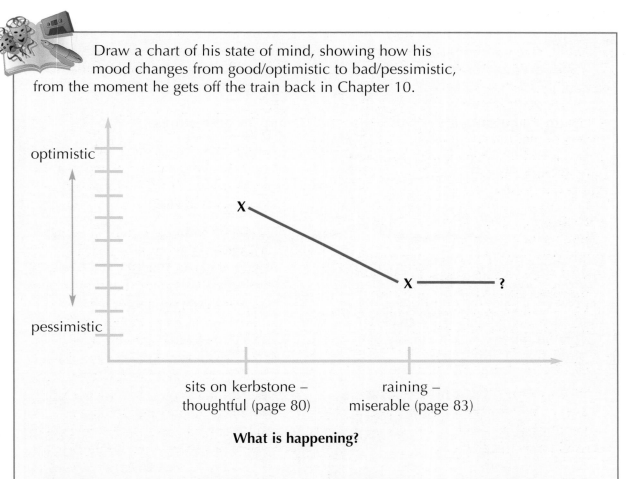

Draw a chart of his state of mind, showing how his mood changes from good/optimistic to bad/pessimistic, from the moment he gets off the train back in Chapter 10.

optimistic

pessimistic

sits on kerbstone –
thoughtful (page 80)

raining –
miserable (page 83)

What is happening?

• Continue adding to this chart as you read on to the end of the story. It is another form of *note-making* to track the development of a character's feelings. Do you prefer it to the other method of making character notes? What do you think are the advantages and disadvantages of each? Which might you use with the next novel you study?

• Alternatively, your group could make these notes on a large wall chart. You can add pictures, or quotations, to this chart. This way you would be able to compare your notes with those of other groups. It would be interesting to see where you disagree with each other.

WHAT WILL HAPPEN NEXT?

Read to the end of Chapter 13. The story sounds like it is ready to end here, as James prepares to return home. Would you be happy to see James' search end here? What questions do you still have? What do you want James to find out or do?

- In groups, write down at least five questions. For example, does James ever find out who his birth mother is?

- Copy the following chart. Once you have agreed on your five questions, write them into the column headed 'Group 1's questions'.

Group 1's questions	Group 2's predictions
1 Does James find out out who his birth mother is?	
2	

- Pass your chart to another group. This group should now discuss and predict answers to the five questions given to them, writing them in the right-hand column. Be prepared to justify your predictions to the class.

- As you read on, see how many of your questions are answered and how accurate your predictions were.

Read on to Chapter 14, up to the point just before James meets the Grandmother to the end of the paragraph beginning "*Can I see your gran?' I asked.'*

- Try to predict what he will find out from her. Then predict what his response to this information will be.

- Justify your ideas. Compare these ideas in a group and then with the whole class.

LOOKING BACK

Read to the end of Chapter 15.

- Early on in this chapter James, referring to his birth mother, writes '*Whatever happens, I thought, I'll keep her secret.*' Why do you think he feels this? Is this the right decision? What would *you* advise him to do?

- Use the information on the pages up to the line '*Somewhere over the other side of it was the house where I was born,*' and what Elizabeth has already written to write a <u>factual recount</u> of James' life up to the point he was handed over to the adoption society. (What you write down is much of the information that James has been searching for.)

  You may need to use the notes you have already made to find some of the references to what happened to James. For example, back at the beginning of Chapter 3 we learnt that

  it was night time

  Elizabeth wrapped the newly-born baby in a sack.

- Work in pairs or small groups to find all the information. It will help if you divide up your roles to look at different parts of the novel. For example, one of you could look for information in Chapter 15; another could look for information in Chapters 13 to 14. Then you can report back to each other to share your findings.

- Remind yourself how to write a factual recount (see the notes on p109).

James tells us what he thinks of Claire. But what does she think of him? And how does the writer want us to respond to each of them?

Imagine Claire writes a diary entry after the events of Chapter 15, when they walk together part of the way up the Tor. You will need to re-read the pages describing them together. (Your notes will help you to find these.) What aspects of his behaviour and personality do you think stand out to her? How does she behave when she is with him? What does this tell you about her feelings towards him? Write Claire's diary entry.

DIARY 1997

James has just left us to look for his birth mother . . . .

CHAPTER 17

Read on to the end of Chapter 17. Do you think you now know enough to write James' family tree? Make a note of all his birth relatives and 'adopted relatives'. You would use this model:

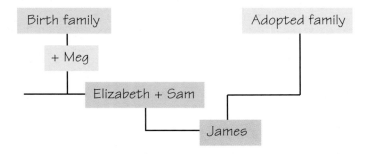

Add information to this as you continue reading. It might help if a large version is written on to a classroom wall chart.

• What about your own family tree? Do you already have one? As a piece of homework research, write your family tree. You will need the help of people at home. Add in dates of births, marriages and deaths. For example:

| Denise (b. 1958) | Michael Jones (b. 1960) m. (1985) Penny Rossiter (b. 1963) |

| Claire (b. 1988) | Luke (b. 1992) | Michelle (b. 1995) |

• As you can see, they can get very complicated! See how far back you can trace your family. Can you get as far back as the nineteenth century?

• If you want to take this a step further, you can find out more about the individuals on your family tree, for example what their jobs were, where they went to school, or even photographs of them.

THE ENDING

Read Chapters 19 to 22. At this point the two stories come together in the barn, as Elizabeth Rowlin looks down at her child in the same place in which he was born fifteen years previously. The scene is described from both James' and Elizabeth's points of view.

What effect do you think Berlie Doherty wanted to have on the reader, by bringing James and Elizabeth together in this way?

In pairs, re-read **the barn scene** and discuss this question. Be prepared to explain your views to another pair. The author's intentions may be clearer if you consider such points as:

• Would it have made a difference to James' story if a different person had come into the barn?

• Would it have made a difference if James had been sleeping in a different building when Elizabeth found him?

Then there is **the river scene**.

What do you think the author wanted to show? Do you think she succeeded?

Again in pairs, re-read this scene and discuss it. It may help if you consider the points on the following page:

[cont...]

- Would the meeting between a boy and his mother really take place like this?

- Is it realistic? Does it have to be realistic anyway?

- Is the setting important?

- Does it add important information to the story? (You could add this to your plot notes.)

- Does it add important information to your understanding of the characters? (You could add this to your character notes.)

Now that you have explored and discussed these two scenes, write down your views.

➡ Organise your thoughts into paragraphs.

➡ Explain yourself clearly, fully, and use plenty of examples.

➡ Pay close attention to spelling and punctuation.

How would _you_ have made James meet his mother?

Write your own alternative version of the meeting. The first important decision you must make is whether to write as though you are James or Elizabeth. Try to write in the style of their writing in the novel.

Before doing so, jot down some ideas on the following:

- _The setting_:
Where would the meeting take place? What kind of atmosphere would this place have? What time of year/day/night? What would the weather be like?

- _The characters_:
Who would be present? Just the two of them? What would they be wearing? What would their facial expressions be when they met? How would they stand/sit? How would they feel? How would they behave? How would they greet, and part from, each other?

- _The dialogue_:
What would they say? What would their voices sound like?

This will test your skills in:

- _reading_: how well you understand the characters

- _writing_: how well can you describe setting, character and motivation through detailed description of places, people and actions.

When you have completed your version of the ending, compare it to other pupils' endings, and then to Berlie Doherty's. Remember, she had to deal with the same problems you have! Has writing your own version given you a better appreciation of how Berlie Doherty wrote hers?

AFTER READING THE BOOK

James is fifteen when he decides to trace his birth mother. In fact, the majority of adopted people do not begin to make enquiries until their mid- to late-twenties. The following accounts are taken from a book called *Preparing for Reunion* .

In pairs or small groups, carefully read these accounts before completing the tasks at the end.

'It is only now, when I feel I've got to the age when I've got all my teenage problems away and I'm fairly secure in myself, that I feel I need to trace my birth mother. I don't regret starting to trace. It is something I thought about over a long period. I feel quite comfortable about it but I have not made contact yet … It is no good going in there because you've got problems at home and expect it is going to be wonderful to have a new family. If you've got problems with one family you have probably got twice as many with two families.'

'I have always known that I was adopted, but always held resentment for my birth parents. I think it was the feeling of not being wanted, rejected, and thinking in a very selfish way that my birth parents could not have really cared about me that much. It was only when I was about 22 that my attitude changed. I had gone through all the changes of life. My adoptive father and only grandparent had died when I was a teenager and my adoptive sister had left home.'

The following account is written by a birth mother and describes her meeting with the daughter whom she had given up for adoption twenty-one years previously.

'On 8 February 1988 an envelope marked O.H.M.S. with a Dunedin postmark arrived through the letter box. I knew what it was after all those years, but I was unprepared for such an unleashing of feelings that overwhelmed me when I opened the letter. There were three – one from the Adult Adoption Information Officer, another from the adoptive mother and finally one from 'my daughter'. I cried solidly for three days and felt as if I were on a high.

It took me three days to answer the letters. Life was unbearable until the reply came – with photographs. I studied them over and over again and could see a likeness to our daughter (aged 14) as a baby, but not to our son (aged 11) nor to me, although my husband said that he could. About three months later when returning from shopping my husband said, 'Your daughter has phoned.' I couldn't believe it, and she later rang back – to make sure I was real, she said! It was wonderful. For the next six months I floated on cloud nine but gradually came down to earth, though I still hung on to every letter. I had also started writing regularly to her adoptive mother, who sounded very nice and extremely supportive and encouraged the contact between us.

Then came the news that she was coming to England to meet me. The time had come to tell our children. We sat down and my husband explained the situation. My daughter immediately understood, as there was a reunion taking place on TV's *Neighbours*. My son said, 'Are there any brothers anywhere?' It really helped and made us laugh. I had also told my mother six months after initial contact was made.

[*continued over...*]

She burst into tears but seemed pleased. My daughter and my cousin arrived at Heathrow in July 1990. It was a nerve-wracking time. I felt sick with worry. Would she like me? Did she look like me? Would she regret coming? It was an emotional meeting. I kept sneaking looks at her as we went back to the car and I just couldn't take it in. She was tired and tearful and slept most of the way home. She was composed meeting my mother and our children until she went up to her room and saw flowers and a big welcome banner, and then it was tears all over again and she said it was something she had dreamed of all her life.

We got along quite well, though it was difficult and to be frank, she got along better with my husband than with me, which I resented. I took her to Scotland for one week to meet my father's family. He had died some years before, but I know that he would have been thrilled to meet her – more so than my mother, who has not told any of her family and friends and sees no point in it.

We talked quite a bit – it wasn't easy and I didn't remember too much especially about the father, as I knew very little and selfishly hoped she didn't want to contact him. I found the whole thing quite stressful but still I was so pleased to have her in my home … The month passed quickly and it was an emotional goodbye at the airport. I hope she found this visit worthwhile. – I did. Whether I would ever have tried to trace I cannot honestly say.'

1. These are **factual** accounts. *The Snake-stone* tells us of a **fictional** account. With your partner, discuss how the following different participants in these factual accounts feel:

- the adopted person

- the birth mother

- the birth mother's husband

- the birth mother's younger children

- the birth mother's mother

Look for key words and expressions that tell us of their emotions (for example: '*unprepared for such an unleashing of feelings that overwhelmed me…*') You may find that some people have a range of different emotions.

2. Now use these ideas to help you with the following task.

Imagine that your best friend has found out that he or she is adopted and is wondering whether to trace and make contact with his or her birth parents. Make a list of all the reasons *for* and *against* taking this action. Try to come up with at least five reasons for each. You could set out your ideas in this way:

For	Against
You might find out that you have other brothers or sisters	You should wait until you are in your 20s

3. Use these notes, and what you learned about the issue of adoption from reading *The Snake-stone*, to write out the conversation you would have with your best friend. Set it out in the form of a playscript. You could then perform it with a partner, either as a piece of live drama, or by recording it.

WHAT NEXT?

In this unit, you have investigated the characters and themes of the novel *The Snake-stone*. You have discussed the central ideas with other members of your group and have written in a variety of formats to show your understanding of the novel and to develop your own skills as a writer.

If you have enjoyed the tasks in the unit you may wish to take your work further.

- James writes a letter to Claire summing up what happened to him and how he feels about these events now, revealing how he has changed during the course of events described in the novel. You will need to consult your character notes to form a clear opinion about how James' character has developed.

    Write this letter. Remember to set it out appropriately for an informal letter. Aim to write in the style that James would use. Begin by jotting down ideas on what you will include. Then write a first draft. Get a critical friend to check this through with you before you redraft it.

- What kind of person is Elizabeth? Read through your character notes to arrive at an opinion. How would you describe her personality? Pick three to five words (for example *brave*), and explain each, giving evidence to support your ideas.

- Imagine a local newspaper hears about James' successful search for his birth mother and decides to run a story on it. James tries to protect his birth mother's identity as a secret, but they manage to get some information from him.

    Write the newspaper article as a front page lead story. What information will you choose to include? Who would the reporters manage to interview to get this information? How much of the information would be accurate, and how much inaccurate (perhaps for the sake of a dramatic story that the readers would want to read)?

    Begin your article with an eye-catching headline. Have a look at a local or tabloid newspaper to see how they present their stories. Usually, the opening paragraph tells the reader most of the information: the Who? What? Where? When? of the story.

- This task is similar to the newspaper one above, but this time the medium is radio or television. A radio or TV station decides to broadcast a programme in which some of the key characters are interviewed about the story. This can be presented to your class either as a live piece of drama, or recorded on to audio or video tape, and then played back to the class.

    See the Help Box on the next page to start you off.

HELP

You will need to consider the following points

CHARACTERS

Decide who to include. You will also need at least one interviewer. What information will each character have to give? Will James try to protect his birth mother's identity, or will she herself be interviewed? Use your plot and character notes to help you find useful information for each character.

SETTING

Where will it take place? On people's doorsteps? In a studio?

SOUND

If you record your interview, will you begin and end the show with theme music? Will you cut for advertisements in the middle? How do radio and television programmes present interviews?

DRAMA SKILLS

Think about (1) body language and (2) how you use your voice, just as you do for any drama or speaking and listening task.

RESEARCH

If you are interested in the topic of adoption, you could use one of the following for some research:

- Internet – search word: 'adoption'

- The Children's Society
  Post Adoption and Care: Counselling and Research Project
  91 Peckham Rd
  London SE15 2EZ

Provides information, advice, counselling and an intermediary service for people adopted through The Children's Society and their relatives.

- TALK adoption –
  freephone 0808 808 1234
  website: www.talkadoption.org.uk

A national helpline for people under 26 who have a link with adoption, whether they are adopted, have given a child for adoption, or are relatives or friends of adopted people.

- The Office for National Statistics
  Adoptions Section
  Contact Register
  Smedley Hydro
  Trafalgar Rd
  Birkdale
  Southport PR8 2HH

Explains how to access birth records.

- The Post Adoption Centre
  5 Torriano Mews
  Torriano Ave
  London NW5 2RZ

A post adoption centre for anyone involved in adoption.

- NORCAP
  112 Church Rd
  Wheatley
  Oxfordshire OX33 1LU

Information for adopted people and both their birth parents and adopted families.

- PPIAS
  Lower Boddington
  Daventry
  Northamptonshire NN11 6YB

Parent to parent information on adoption services.

Before you begin to research a topic, answer the questions in the first row on the table below. On a separate sheet, create a table like this and complete it by making notes to answer the questions.

1. What do I want to find out?	2. Where will I find this information?	3. What do I already know about this topic?	4. How will I record my findings?

HELP

Question 1:
This may be to locate a single answer to a single question (e.g. *How many adoptions took place in the UK in 2000?*), or a series of questions, all of which need answers, or a single but broader question (e.g. *What does it feel like for an adopted person to find her birth mother?*)

Question 2:
You could try:
- the Internet
- non-fiction texts in the library
- leaflets
- a questionnaire
- interviewing people.

Question 4:
You could consider the following:
- making written notes
- tape or video recordings
- taking photographs.

UNIT SIX

Our Changing Language

In this unit, you will learn about the way in which the English language has changed since its early days – and is still changing. You will develop your skills as:

SPEAKERS & LISTENERS

by helping each other to solve problems in a logical way
by working together to produce a whole-class wall display

READERS

by close study of a range of writing from the past 1000 years
by looking at the ways in which words and sentences are put together
by researching relevant information in reference books

WRITERS

by writing to explain how the changes in our language have happened
by contributing to a whole-class wall display

When you turn the page, you will see a piece of writing in English which dates back over a thousand years. In groups of two or three, try to read through the text, seeing if you can figure out what some of the words mean. You may then be able to guess what it is that you are reading.

Fæder ure, þu þe eart on
heofonum, si þin nama
gehalgod.
Tobecume þin rice. Gewurþe ðin
willa on earðan swa swa on
heofonum.
Urne gedæghwamlican hlaf syle
us to-dæg.
And forgyf us ure gyltas swa swa
we forgyfað urum gyltendum.
And ne gelæd þu us on
costnunge, ac alys us of yfele.

(about 1000 AD)

Now that you have read through this text, you may have a general idea of the meaning, because you have already guessed what it is. See if you can work out the meanings of words and phrases in more detail. Can you explain some of the ways in which the language used is like our language today? In what ways is it different?

SIMILARITIES AND DIFFERENCES

Get together in groups of three or four.

- When you have found out what this (well-known!) piece of writing is, write out your own translation (or ask your teacher to give you a translation).

HELP

Remember what you have learnt about dealing with unfamiliar texts.

See what words you **can** recognize. Don't be put off by the spelling. If you try to say the words aloud, you'll probably see that many words are like our Modern English words.

Break the words down into **syllables**. Look for the **roots** of words see if there is a modern word which sounds similar.

When you've worked out which words you recognise, try to work out the words which would fit in between them. Have a go!

- Try to work out, as far as you can, what **each word** in this text means.

- Then sort out the similarities and differences that you can spot between this Old English text, written down in the 11th Century, and how it would be written in Modern English. Make notes, on a separate sheet, answering the following questions:

What words can you recognize, even though the spelling is different?

What words have now dropped completely out of our modern language?

How is the word-order of sentences different from Modern English?

- Discuss your findings with your teacher and the rest of your class, recording what you have learnt about Old English in your notebook.

- Finally, write two paragraphs in your notebook, one about the differences between Old English and Modern English, and one about the similarities.

WHO SPOKE OLD ENGLISH?

Old English is an early version of our language and was spoken by tribes of people who came from Northern Germany. The map shows you where they came from, and the parts of the country where each tribe settled.

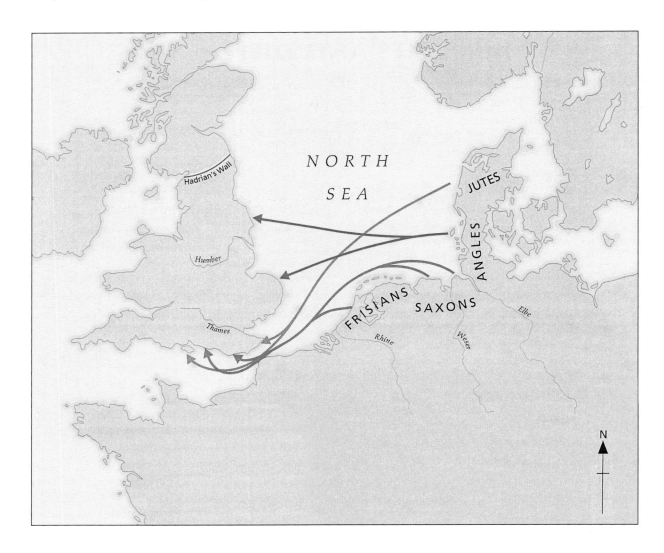

The invaders took over the country gradually, arriving in groups over a period of many years from around the middle of the 5th Century AD. They settled increasingly large areas, and drove out the Romano-British who had lived there for nearly 1000 years. The British called all the invaders 'Saxons', no matter what tribe they came from. By the end of the 6th Century AD, the invaders were called 'Angles' or 'Engles'. You can see how the Old English adjective 'Englisc' came to describe the language, and how the country eventually became known as 'Englaland'.

- Begin a time-line from 500AD to 2000AD. As you work through this unit, make sure that you note down, on your time-line, any major events in the story of our changing language. What will your first entries be?

WHERE DID THESE INVADERS SETTLE?

Although the language the invaders spoke was known as 'English', they were in fact different tribes who had come from different parts of Northern Germany. Each tribe settled in a different part of the country, as the map on page 130 showed. Each tribe had a different way of speaking English, but they could still understand each other. These different ways of speaking are called **dialects**. The map below shows the main dialect areas, with the names of local tribes and kingdoms.

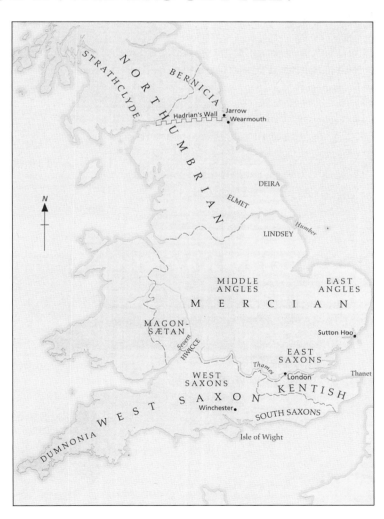

Even in our Modern English dialects – the different ways we speak in different parts of the country – we can still tell which of the tribes from Germany settled the area where we live or where our family come from.

- How does the dialect of your own area differ from other parts of the country? How does the dialect of your own area differ from Standard English? Share your ideas in groups, then as a whole class, start to build up a picture of your dialect.

- When you have collected your examples in groups and as a class, try to explain the ways in which the dialect speech of your area is different from other parts of country and from Standard English. Write a paragraph in your notebook explaining what you have found out, making sure you give plenty of examples. Remember that people in your area talk like they do partly because of the Germanic tribe that settled in your part of the country about 1500 years ago!

HELP

Standard English is a dialect used throughout the country, not just in one part of it.

It is the dialect that books are written in. It is, therefore, the language of schools and universities. It is also the language of professions which need a high level of education.

To speak and write Standard English as well as speaking a regional dialect gives you more power and opportunities than if you only spoke or wrote a local version of English. That's why you are taught Standard English in school!

ANOTHER INVASION

In 1066, a date everyone knows, William the Conqueror led the Norman invasion of England, defeated the English King, Harold, and marched on London to take control of the government.

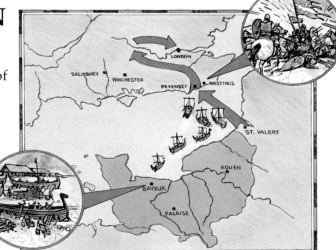

William replaced the English courtiers, nobility, judges and churchmen with his own followers. He fought battles against the English nobility and landowners, and gave their estates to those who had fought alongside him. William's followers were all French speakers, and so it was natural for them to use their own language, not the language of the defeated English.

But, strangely, English survived. Here is a description of what happened to the language after the Norman Conquest. It was written in about 1300 by a historian called Robert of Gloucester:

Thus came England into Normandy's hand.
And the Normans didn't know how to speak then but their own speech
And spoke French as they did at home, and their children did also teach;
So that high men of this land, that of their blood come,
Hold all that same speech, that they took from them.
For, but a man know French, men count of him little.
But low men hold to English, and to their own speech, yet.
I think that there are, in all the world, no countries
That don't hold to their own speech, but England alone.
But men know well that it is well for to know both,
For the more that a man knows, the more worth he is.

The spelling of this text has been updated. The word-order is not the same as Modern English though. It is similar in many ways to the Old English which you read earlier. The meaning of some common words has changed, and sometimes you have to think carefully about who the pronouns refer back to.

- Working in small groups, rewrite in Modern English what Robert of Gloucester is saying.

- Why do you think 'low men' held onto their own speech, despite the importance of French?

- When you have shared your ideas with the rest of your class, bring your time-lines up to date, and write one or two paragraphs in your notebooks, explaining what happened to English after the Norman Conquest.

GLOSSARY

Thus - in this way
Then - at that time
But - only
Blood - background, family
Hold - think, consider, believe
But - unless
Count of - value
Low - lower class
Hold - hang on to

WORDS THE FRENCH GAVE US

As you can imagine, the invasion changed our language very much. Without the French take-over, we would probably talk today in a way close to modern Dutch or German. One thing the Norman Conquest gave us though, was a huge number of new words. Here are some of them:

accuse	chant	defence	jewel	ornament	saint
administer	chimney		joist		salad
anatomy	clergy	enemy	judgement	paper	soldier
army	coat		jury	park	spice
authority	collar	feast	justice	parliament	stomach
	combat	frock		pastry	story
battle	complaint		leisure	poem	study
biscuit	convert	geometry	literature	pulse	sugar
button	convict	grammar	logic		surgeon
	council	guard		rhyme	
	court		mansion		toast
	cream	image	marriage		tournament
	curtain		medicine		
			music		
			mystery		

- Look up in a dictionary the meaning of any words on this list that you don't know.

- Separate the list into the categories shown, in a table like the one below.

Art/learning/medicine	
Church/religion	
Fashion/food/social life	
Government	
Law	
Warfare	

- Can you explain why the French gave us so many words in these categories?

- All the words on the list above are nouns. Using an etymological dictionary, can you find a range of adjectives and nouns that come from French? Could you fit them into the categories above, or will you need new categories?

- What are you going to add to your time-line? When you have decided, write two paragraphs explaining how the French contributed to our range of vocabulary after the Conquest.

THE REBIRTH OF ENGLISH

Gradually, English took over from French as the language of the upper class. About 300 years after the Norman conquest, English was again the language of the court, but we call it 'Middle English', because it was different in many ways from Old English.

Here are two examples of what it looked like at that time. The first example is from 'Sir Gawaine and the Green Knight', which you came across in the version told by Hugh Lupton in Unit One:

Wel gay watȝ þis gome gered in grene,
And þe here of his hed of his hors swete.
Fayre fannand fax vmbefoldes his schulderes;
A much berd as a busk ouer his brest henges,

Bot in his on honde he hade a holyn bobbe,
And an ax in his oþer, a hoge and vnmete,
A spetos sparþe to expoun in spelle, quoso myȝt.

G L O S S A R Y	G L O S S A R Y	G L O S S A R Y	G L O S S A R Y
Gay	brightly	*on*	one
Gome	knight	*honde*	hand
Gered	clothed	*holyn bobbe*	bunch of holly
Of his hors swete	to match his horse	*hoge*	huge
Fayre	handsome	*unmete*	monstrous
Fannand	spreading out like a fan	*spetos*	cruel
Fax	hair	*sparthe*	battle-axe
Umbefoldes	enfolds, drapes over	*expoun*	describe
Much	enormous	*spelle*	speech
Busk	bush	*quoso*	whosoever
		myȝt	might

- Working in groups, work out what these extracts from the description of the Green Knight mean.

- Remember how you worked out the meaning of the Old English text. Read words aloud, and see how they sound close to Modern English words. Break words down into syllables. Look for word roots.

- Now list similarities and differences between this example of Middle English, and the Old English at the start of this unit. Look at word order as well as words, spellings and meanings.

- In what ways is it similar to, and different from, Modern English?

Nobody knows who the writer of 'Sir Gawain and the Green Knight' was, although he probably lived and wrote in the North-West Midlands, towards the River Mersey. The poem was written before 1400. Geoffrey Chaucer (1345–1400), who is seen as the first great writer in English, was also writing at around the same time as the 'Gawain' poet. Here he is describing a miller, who is one of a group of pilgrims going to Canterbury.

The MILLERE was a stout carl for the nones;
Ful big he was of brawn, and eek of bones.
That proved wel, for over al ther he cam,
At wrastlinge he wolde have alwey the ram.
He was short-sholdered, brood, a thikke knarre;
Ther was no dore that he nolde heve of harre,
Or breke it at a renning with his heed.
His berd as any sowe or fox was reed,
And therto brood, as though it were a spade.
Upon the cop right of his nose he hade
A werte, and theron stood a toft of heris,
Reed as the brustles of a sowes eris;
His nosethirles blake were and wide.

- In pairs, work out what Chaucer is saying in each line.

- List the ways in which this extract is closer to Modern English than the lines by the 'Gawain' poet.

GLOSSARY   GLOSSARY   GLOSSARY   GLOSSARY

Carl	a man, especially one who is common, or rough in manners	*Thikke*	(Be careful with this. It **doesn't** mean 'stupid'.)
For the nones	really, indeed	*Knarre*	hard man
Brawn	muscles	*Nolde*	would not
Eek	also	*Harre*	hinges
Over al ther	wherever	*Renning*	running
Cam	went, travelled	*Cop*	top
The ram	the prize in a wrestling competition	*Werte*	wart
		Heris	hairs
		Thirles	holes

DEVELOPING STANDARD ENGLISH

The two texts you have just been reading were both written at about the same time, but the kinds of English they are using are very different. Which one is closer to today's Standard English? List your reasons.

The reason for the difference between these two versions of English is that, at the time, there wasn't a standard form of the language. Here are some facts about Chaucer and the 'Gawain' poet, and about the times they lived in:

Chaucer lived in London, and was well-known at the royal court in London. The 'Gawain' poet lived in the North-West Midlands and we have very little information about him. The main law courts were in London, and the King's Chancery was also situated there. The Chancery was set up in the 12th Century to keep royal records in a systematic way. The scribes who wrote and copied documents were trained to use a common system of handwriting, spelling and grammar. They produced a vast number of documents, which were widely spread throughout the country. William Caxton set up the first printing press in this country in London, in 1476, near the royal court and the Chancery. At the time, London was at the centre of a wealthy area, with many immigrants moving to London, because of its wealth. London is also close to the ancient universities of Oxford and Cambridge.

William Caxton presenting printed book to Queen

- What does this information tell you about the factors which are needed to produce a standard dialect?

- When you have discussed these factors, write two paragraphs explaining how Standard English developed. Don't forget to update your time-line.

EARLY MODERN ENGLISH

By the time we reach Shakespeare (1564–1616), the language is very close to Modern English. There is a mainly-standard written language, spread through printing. However, there are still some differences from Modern English that can be seen in the grammar. Punctuation in Shakespeare's time was moving away from the old usage where it indicated pauses. It was moving towards the modern usage, to mark the sentences, clauses and phrases in a text. The punctuation in the extract which follows has been modernised. Spelling was not yet fully standardised, and has also been mainly modernised.

This speech comes from one of Shakespeare's most famous plays, *Hamlet*. The events take place at the King's castle in Denmark. Hamlet, the prince, is visiting his home following the funeral of his father (who had also been called Hamlet). Hamlet's father died in very mysterious circumstances, and there are rumours that his ghost has been seen on the castle's battlements. Hamlet decides to spend the night watching, to see if the ghost will appear. And then, suddenly, it does…

> ***HAMLET***
> Angels and ministers of grace defend us!
> Be thou a spirit of health or goblin damned,
> Bring with thee airs from heaven or blasts from hell,
> Be thy intents wicked or charitable,
> Thou com'st in such a questionable shape
> That I will speak to thee. I'll call thee Hamlet,
> King, father, royal Dane. Oh answer me!
> Let me not burst in ignorance, but tell
> Why thy canonised bones, hearsed in death,
> Have burst their cerements, why thy sepulchre
> Wherein we saw thee quietly enurned
> Hath oped his ponderous and marble jaws
> To cast thee up again. What may this mean,
> That thou, dead corse, again in complete steel,
> Revisits thus the glimpses of the moon,
> Making night hideous?

Hamlet, Act 1, Scene 4, lines 20–35

GLOSSARY GLOSSARY GLOSSARY GLOSSARY

ministers of grace	ministers of the church, priests
damned	doomed to go to hell
charitable	kind hearted
canonised bones	
hearsed in death	a body which has been buried in a religious ceremony
cerements	grave clothes
sepulchre	a burial vault or tomb
enurned	buried, laid to rest
ponderous	heavy
corse	corpse, dead body

- In groups, read through this speech and discuss what it means. Use a dictionary to check the meaning of words you don't know. What punctuation marks are used? Tally the number of times each mark is used and explain what it is there for. How does the punctuation help with performing the speech aloud?

- One difference in Shakespeare's grammar from Modern English is the way he uses the pronouns 'thou', 'thee' and 'thy'. What do these words mean, and where do you find them in sentences? What verb suffix goes with 'thou'?

- He also writes 'Let me not burst in ignorance…' How would we write this today?

One of Shakespeare's greatest contributions to changing our language was the number of new words which he invented. He was also one of the earliest users of many words which had just come into the language at a time of great change and inventiveness. In this speech alone, there are two words for which he is the first recorded user ('cerements' and 'enurned'). There are also two for which he is only the second recorded user ('questionable' and 'hearsed'). We will return later to the ways in which new words enter our language.

- What will you add to your time-line? Write two or three paragraphs explaining Shakespeare's contribution to our changing language and the ways in which his language is still different from Modern English.

STANDARDISING SPELLING

In 1755, Dr Samuel Johnson finished his dictionary. He said that when he was planning his great work, he found our language to be 'without order, and… without rules'. His job, as he saw it, was to 'disentangle perplexity' and to 'regulate confusion' in the language by writing his dictionary. He was not the first person to think about doing this. For example, Richard Mulcaster, in 1582, wrote:

'It were a thing verie praiseworthie… if som one well learned…wold gather all the words which we use in our English tung…into one dictionarie.'

However, Dr Johnson was the first to put a dictionary together in a way that we recognise as modern.

DICTIONARIES NOW AND THEN

To the left is a page from Dr Johnson's dictionary. Compare it with the modern school dictionary on the next page.

ETE

will not obey, who, to get rid of his rider, rifes mightily before; and while his forehand is yet in the air, yerks furioufly with his hind legs. *Farrier's Dict.*

ESTRE'ATE. *n. f.* [*extractum*, Latin.] The true copy of an original writing: for example, of amerciaments or penalties, fet down in the rolls of a court, to be levied by the bailiff, or other officer, of every man for his offence. A law term. *Cowel.*

ESTRE'PEMENT. *n. f.* [of the French word *eftre, ier.*] Spoil made by the tenant for term of life upon any lands or woods, to the prejudice of him in the reverfion. *Cowel.*

E'STRICH. *n. f.* [commonly written *oftrich.*] The largeft of birds.

> To be furious,
> Is to be frighted out of fear; and, in that mood,
> The dove will peck the *eftridge. Shak Anth. and Cleopatra.*
> The peacock, not at thy command, affumes
> His glorious train; nor *eftrich* her rare plumes. *Sandys.*

E'STUARY. *n. f.* [*æftuarium*, Latin.] An arm of the fea; the mouth of a lake or river in which the tide reciprocates; a frith.

To E'STUATE. *v. a.* [*æftuo*, Latin.] To fwell and fall reciprocally; to boil; to be in a ftate of violent commotion. *Dict.*

ESTUA'TION. *n. f.* [from *æftuo*, Latin.] The ftate of boiling; reciprocation of rife and fall; agitation; commotion.

> Rivers and lakes, that want fermenting parts at the bottom, are not excited unto *eftuations*; therefore fome feas flow higher than others. *Brown's Vulgar Errours, b. vii. c. 13.*
> The motion of the will is accompanied with a fenfible commotion of the fpirits, and an *eftuation* of the blood. *Norris.*

E'STURE. *n. f.* [*æftus*, Latin.] Violence; commotion.

> The feas retain
> Not only their outrageous *efture* there,
> But fupernatural mifchief they expire. *Chapman's Odyffey.*

E'SURIENT. *adj.* [*efuriens*, Latin.] Hungry; voracious. *Dict.*

E'SURINE. *adj.* [*efurio*, Latin.] Corroding; eating.

> Over much piercing is the air of Hampftead, in which fort of air there is always fomething *efurine* and acid. *Wifeman.*

ETC. A contraction of the two Latin words *et cætera*, which fignifies *and fo on; and the reft; and others of the like kind.*

To ETCH. *v. a.* [*etizen*, German.]

1. A way ufed in making of prints, by drawing with a proper needle upon a copper-plate, covered over with a ground of wax, &c. and well blacked with the fmoke of a link, in order to take off the figure of the drawing or print; which having its backfide tinctured with white lead, will, by running over the ftrucken out lines with a ftift, imprefs the exact figure on the black or red ground; which figure is afterwards with needles drawn deeper quite through the ground, and all the fhadows and hatchings put in; and then a wax border being made all round the plate, there is poured on a fufficient quantity of well tempered *aqua fortis*, which, infinuating into the ftrokes made by the needles, ufually eats, in about half an hour, into the figure of the print or drawing on the copper plate. *Harris.*

2. To fcetch; to draw; to delineate [unlefs this word be miftaken by *Locke* for *eke.*]

> There are many empty terms to be found in fome learned writers, to which they had recourfe to *etch* out their fyftems. *Locke.*

3. [This word is evidently miftaken by *Ray* for *edge.*] To move forwards towards one fide.

> When we lie long awake in the night, we are not able to reft one quarter of an hour without fhifting of fides, or at leaft *etching* this way and that way, more or lefs. *Ray.*

ETCH. *n. f.* A country word, of which I know not the meaning.

> When they fow their *etch* crops, they fprinkle a pound or two of clover on an acre. *Mortimer's Hufbandry.*
> Where you find dunging of land makes it rank, lay dung upon the *etch*, and fow it with barley. *Mortimer's Hufbandry.*

estuary, **estuaries** (pronounced **est**-yoo-ree) (noun)
An estuary is the wide part of a river near where it joins the sea and where fresh water mixes with salt water.

etc. a written abbreviation for **et cetera**.

et cetera (pronounced it **set**-ra)
Et cetera is used at the end of a list to indicate that other items of the same type you have mentioned could have been mentioned if there had been time or space.
[From Latin *et cetera* meaning 'and other things']

etch, **etches**, **etching**, **etched**
1 (verb) If you etch a design or pattern on a surface, you cut it into the surface by using acid or a sharp tool.
2 If something is etched on your mind or memory, it has made such a strong impression on you that you feel you will never forget it.
etched (adjective).

etching, **etchings**
(noun) An etching is a picture printed from a metal plate that has had a design cut into it.

eternal
(adjective) lasting forever, or seeming to last forever, e.g. *his eternal grumbling*.
eternally (adverb)

Similar words: perpetual, everlasting, endless

eternity, **eternities**
1 (noun) Eternity is time without end, or a state of existing outside time, especially the state some people believe they will pass into when they die.
2 An eternity is also a period of time which seems to go on for ever, e.g. *This winter seems to have lasted for an eternity!*

ether (pronounced **eeth**-er)
1 (noun) Ether is a colourless liquid that burns easily. It is used in industry as a solvent and in medicine as an anaesthetic.
2 (a literary or formal use) The ether is the air.

ethereal, (pronounced ith-**ee**-ree-al)
(adjective) light and delicate, e.g. *her ethereal beauty*.

From *Collins School Dictionary* pp247–248.

- In groups, list the features of Dr Johnson's method of explaining words. Look at the kind of information he gives the reader about each word. How many of these features appear in the modern dictionary?

- How many of the same words appear in both dictionaries? Why is there a difference between the words that have been included?

- Can you summarise what Dr Johnson wanted to do with the language?

- What are the advantages and disadvantages of what he was proposing?

- What do you think was the effect of his dictionary on language change, and on Standard English?

- Bring your time-line up to date, and write one or two paragraphs explaining how Dr Johnson contributed to our changing language.

OUR LANGUAGE – STILL CHANGING!

Modern English has changed a lot from the Old English you studied at the beginning of this unit. However, it is still, basically, the same language. Nowadays though, we have a standard written version of grammar and spelling. These aspects of the language don't seem to be changing very much, but change is still going on in spoken English, and in vocabulary.

In spoken English, the accent of South East England is spreading more widely. This accent has been called 'Estuary English'. Can you explain why it is called that? What do you think is causing it to spread?

NEW WORDS FOR OLD

The vocabulary of English is changing rapidly. Here are some examples of ways in which words are created in English.

- *Does your laptop have a CD-ROM?* The underlined word is called an **acronym**. Can you work out what an acronym is? Can you think of any more examples?

- *She left her handbag on the train.* This is an example of **compounding**. Again, can you explain how the word has been created? Can you think of other examples of compounding?

- **Shortening** is another method of word-creation. For example, *phone* has been shortened from *telephone*. Can you think of other examples of shortening?

- *Telephone* itself, and *television*, have both been created by **affixation**. So have *kindness*, *supervisor* and *successful*. Try breaking the words down into the parts that they are made from. This will help you work out how words are built up with **affixes**. Again, can you think of other examples?

- Finally, there is a method called **conversion**. You find it in sentences like *He downed his glass of coke quickly* or *The builders bricked up the doorway*. What has happened to the underlined words? Think of what word class they are now, and what class the original words were. Can you find other examples of conversion?

- Now work in pairs to write a dictionary definition of each word-creation method. Use what you have learnt about dictionaries earlier in the unit.

THAT'S A NICE WORD. MAY I BORROW IT, PLEASE?

What the English language is outstanding at, is borrowing words from other languages. Here is a small (100-word) sample of the words which we have borrowed since Shakespeare's time.

agile	concerto	hurricane	photon	tobacco
allergy	contradictory		pneumonia	toboggan
alligator	cork	invite	potato	tortilla
anonymous	crisis curry		port (wine)	trek
anorak		jaguar	puma	tycoon
antiseptic	detail	jungle	pyjamas	
armada	dingo			vacuum
atmosphere	disability	landscape	relaxation	violin
	duel	lunar	robot	virus
banana				vitamin
barricade	easel	kamikaze	safari	volcano
benefit	emphasis	karaoke	shampoo	
bizarre	encyclopaedia	kayak	sherry	whiskey
boomerang	enthusiasm	kung fu	skeleton	wigwam
bungalow	exact		sketch	
	exaggerate	macaroni	ski	yacht
canoe	expectation	mosquito	solo	yoga
carnival	explain		soprano	
centigrade		obstruction	system	
chipmunk	fact	opera		
chocolate	fuselage	oxygen	tattoo	
chutney		pancreas	tea	
cockroach	glottis	parka	temperature	
cocoa	grotto	passport	thermometer	
comrade	guitar	pasteurize	ticket	

- Working in groups, find out the meaning of any word on this list which you don't know.

- Using an etymological dictionary, find out what language each of these words comes from. Try also to identify the place in the world where each word originates.

- Can you put these words into categories? Does that help you to explain how and why borrowings come into our language?

- Look back over your work in this unit. How many other influences on language change have you come across?

WHAT NEXT?

In this unit you have thought about the ways in which the English language has changed over the past 1500 years. You have read examples of Old, Middle and Modern English, and looked at how they differ. You have looked at the development of Standard English and why it is important. You have also written paragraphs explaining what you have learnt in a logical way.

To bring the unit to a conclusion, everybody in the group should take part in the first activity, or contribute to it with one of the two choices which come afterwards:

• Drawing on your own time-lines and the paragraphs you have written, everyone should contribute to a whole-wall time-line. It should start at 500AD and finish at 2000AD. Mark the main events in the story of our changing language. Draft your paragraphs and stick them onto the right place on the time-line. Include maps and illustrations. Make it colourful and ensure that your handwriting, spelling and punctuation are the best. Think about your personal targets. Particular groups may wish to have responsibility for particular parts of the display. You should discuss this with your teacher.

Here are two other possibilities for individual work, which may be contributed to the display:

• Using what you have learnt, write a feature article, called 'Our Changing Language', for a magazine of your choice. You will need to discuss with your teacher the style of the magazine, so that you can write your own article in the same way.

• Investigate the place names in your local area. What languages do they come from? What do they tell you about the countryside over 1000 years ago, and about the people who lived where you do now?

Poetry in Performace

In this unit, you will learn how to bring poetry to life, and improve your skills as:

SPEAKERS AND LISTENERS

by performing a selection of poetry
by discussing your views and ideas about poetry

READERS

by looking at a wide variety of poetry
by responding to the styles, language and themes in a range of poetry

WRITERS

by recording your thoughts about different poems
by making notes on useful techniques and writing journal entries

Think back to the first forms of poetry you ever learned: nursery rhymes, songs from the charts, skipping songs, etc. Perhaps you know a very young child who is learning the same verses even now? Discuss your thoughts with a friend and then begin your poetry journey…

SKIPPING SONG

Ann and Belinda
Turning the rope
Helen jumps in
But she hasn't got a hope
Helen Freckles
What will you do
Skip on the table
In the Irish stew
Freckles on her face
Freckles on her nose
Freckles on her bum
Freckles on her toes
Helen Freckles
Tell me true
How many freckles
Have you got on you
One two three four five six seven
And out goes you.

Stella Starwars
Skip in soon
Into your spaceship
And off to the moon
Skip on the pavement
One and two
Skip like a rabbit
Or a kangaroo
Skip so high
You never come down
Over the steeples
Over the town
Skip over rooftops
Skip over trees
Skip over rivers
Skip over seas
Skip over London
Skip over Rome
Skip all night
And never come home
Skip over moonbeams
Skip over Mars
Skip through the Milky Way
And try to count the stars
One two three four five six seven
Out goes you.

Gareth Owen

ROPE RHYME

Get set, ready now, jump right in
Bounce and kick and giggle and spin
Listen to the rope when it hits the ground
Listen to that clappedy-slappedy sound
Jump right up when it tells you to
Come back down whatever you do
Count to a hundred, count by ten
Start to count all over again
That's what jumping is all about
Get set, ready now,
jump
        right
                out!

Eloise Greenfield

SKIPPING SONGS

While children skip, they often chant rhymes which match the rhythm of the rope turning.

- As a class, read the poem by Gareth Owen. Stand in a circle and read a line each around the circle until all of the lines are read. Try to keep the rhythm of a turning skipping rope.

- Think of a different way to read the other poem. For example, someone could beat a drum to give the steady rhythm while the poems are being read.

- What other types of poems can you think of which have a strong rhythm like skipping songs?

USING PUNCTUATION

Watch out for punctuation when you read a poem. Commas, colons, semi-colons, dashes and full stops all tell you to pause. Question marks and exclamation marks advise you about how a line should sound. Speech marks show you that your voice should change to reflect a character's speech.

- Read through the poem on the following page, 'Macavity: the Mystery Cat', and spend a few minutes writing down your thoughts. What could you see/hear/feel when you read it? What did it make you think of? What were the words/phrases/rhythms/rhymes which attracted your attention?

MACAVITY: THE MYSTERY CAT

Macavity's a Mystery Cat: he's called the Hidden Paw –
For he's the master criminal who can defy the Law.
He's the bafflement of Scotland Yard, the Flying Squad's despair:
For when they reach the scene of crime – *Macavity's not there!*

Macavity, Macavity, there's no one like Macavity,
He's broken every human law, he breaks the law of gravity.
His powers of levitation would make a fakir stare,
And when you reach the scene of crime – *Macavity's not there!*
You may see him in the basement, you may look up in the air –
But I tell you once and once again, *Macavity's not there!*

Macavity's a ginger cat, he's very tall and thin;
You would know him if you saw him, for his eyes are sunken in.
His brow is deeply lined with thought, his head is highly domed;
His coat is dusty from neglect, his whiskers are uncombed.
He sways his head from side to side, with movements like a snake;
And when you think he's half asleep, he's always wide awake.

Macavity, Macavity, there's no one like Macavity,
For he's a fiend in feline shape, a monster of depravity.
You may meet him in a by-street, you may see him in the square –
But when a crime's discovered, then *Macavity's not there!*

He's outwardly respectable. (They say he cheats at cards.)
And his footprints are not found in any file of Scotland Yard's.
And when the larder's looted, or the jewel-case is rifled,
Or when the milk is missing, or another Peke's been stifled,
Or the greenhouse glass is broken, and the trellis past repair –
Ay, there's the wonder of the thing! *Macavity's not there!*

And when the Foreign Office find a Treaty's gone astray,
Or the Admiralty lose some plans and drawings by the way,
There may be a scrap of paper in the hall or on the stair –
But it's useless to investigate – *Macavity's not there!*
And when the loss has been disclosed, the Secret Service say:
"It *must* have been Macavity!" – but he's a mile away.

You'll be sure to find him resting, or a-licking of his thumbs,
Or engaged in doing complicated long division sums.

Macavity, Macavity, there's no one like Macavity,
There never was a Cat of such deceitfulness and suavity.
He always has an alibi, and one or two to spare:
At whatever time the deed took place – *MACAVITY WASN'T THERE*!
And they say that all the Cats whose wicked deeds are widely known
(I might mention Mungojerrie, I might mention Griddlebone)
Are nothing more than agents for the Cat who all the time
Just controls their operations: the Napoleon of Crime!

T. S. Eliot

USING PUNCTUATION

- How many different punctuation marks can you spot in this poem? Work with a partner and count the number of times each mark is used.

- Again, working with a partner, remind yourself of the rules for using each of these punctuation marks. Can you find any places where the writer breaks these rules? Can you explain why he does this?

- Now divide into seven groups to prepare for reading 'Macavity' aloud. Each group should take charge of reading one of the sections or verses of the poem. In your small group, take it in turns to read until you reach a punctuation mark, then stop for the next person to carry on. Continue doing this around your group until you reach the end of your verse. Rehearse your reading several times. Now, all of the groups join together again to perform a reading of the whole poem.

- You have looked at how writers use rhythm in skipping songs and other poems. There is a strong rhythm in 'Macavity: the Mystery Cat.' Try reading a few lines while a partner taps the rhythm. Decide which beats are the strongest ones. In your group, discuss any effects the rhythm has and any reasons you can think of why the poet uses this rhythm.

THE LOOKER-ON

...And ladders leaning against damson trees,
And idle spades beside old garden walls,
And broken sickles covered up in leaves,
And baskets wet with dew, waist deep in grass,
And spider webs across half-open gates...
   And memory of a moon, a giant rolling,
And, brown in moon's noonday, prolific oaks,
Glint of moonsilver on their solid acorns...
   And a fierce sun melting the fringed horizon,
Cold grass, hard apples fallen and forgotten,
And dew-logged thistledown... And crackling beechmast,
And plump matt mushrooms – beggars' harvest – white
As chalk, bland as a nut, and pink to break...
   And bonfire incense, and bracken gold as beech,
And bearded hedges, latest blackberries,
Half-ploughed stubble and dusty threshing yards,
And early nights, cloud multitudes on fire...
Dry noons, drenched dawns, deep scents, bright starts, lost thoughts...
   And empty orchards and wide open fields,
And robin solos in deserted woods,
And chimney smoke, and starry candlelight,
And far-off fields, and distance like the past,
And mossy silence, and the scent of leisure,
And spider webs across half-open gates,
And broken sickles buried under leaves,
And idle spades beside old garden walls,
And ladders leaning against damson trees...

Frank Kendon

CHOOSING AND USING WORDS

A poem can paint a picture of a scene by selecting details and building them up, line by line. The sounds of the words and the way they are put together help to build up the atmosphere.

BUILDING AN IMAGE

- As a class, sit in a circle. Take it in turns around the circle to read 'The Looker-on' until you reach the word 'and' – then hand over the reading to the next person. Some of you will need to read two lines, whilst others will only need to read a phrase. Remember to pause at a punctuation mark. Think about how you want your line(s) to sound.

- Discuss the effect created by the poet continually repeating 'and'. Why do you think he does this?

- Choose one of the following phrases from the poem – it should be the one you like most. Copy the phrase into your journal, thinking carefully about each word. Draw a picture showing what the phrase makes you imagine.

  'idle spades'
  'broken sickles'
  'glint of moonsilver'
  'plump matt mushrooms'
  'bearded hedges'
  'distance like the past'
  'dry noons, drenched dawns, deep scents, bright stars, lost thoughts...'
  'mossy silence'

- Write your answers to the questions below, in as much detail as you can.

  1 What does your phrase actually describe?

  2 What impressions does it give you of the whole atmosphere beyond what it actually describes?

  3 Is there anything unusual, appealing or striking about the words in the phrase you have chosen? How do they work together and why do you think the poet chose them?

- Now read the following poem. Before moving on to the activities, spend some time writing in your journal to capture your first impressions.

I have walked a great while over the snow,
And I am not tall nor strong.
My clothes are wet, and my teeth are set,
And the way was hard and long.
I have wandered over the fruitful earth,
But I never came here before.
Oh, lift me over the threshold,
        and let me in at the door!

The cutting wind is a cruel foe.
I dare not stand in the blast.
My hands are stone, and my voice a groan,
And the worst of death is past.
I am but a little maiden still,
My little white feet are sore.
Oh, lift me over the threshold,
        and let me in at the door!

Her voice was the voice that women have,
Who plead for their heart's desire.
She came – she came – and the quivering flame
Sank and died in the fire.
It never was lit again on my hearth
Since I hurried across the floor,
To lift her over the threshold,
        and let her in at the door.

Mary Coleridge

CREATING AN ATMOSPHERE

- Read the poem a few times, and on a clean sheet of paper (or in your exercise book), make notes on:
  - Any questions the poem raises in your mind.
  - Any phrases or lines you like, and why.
  - Who is speaking in each of the verses.
  - What you find out about characters.
  - The third verse hints that something happens after the visitor is let into the house. What do you think this might have been?
  - What clues are there in the poem that tell you it was written over a hundred years ago?

- Compare your notes with a partner's notes, and discuss the points together.
  Make a list of the ways in which you think the atmosphere of mystery is created.

- Think up possible ideas for a suitable title. Choose one that seems to fit the poem best. Present your title to your group and give your reasons.

- Perform a reading of the poem, either to the whole class, on tape, or to a video camera, drawing out the mystery and strangeness in the poem. Notice which words have the most effect and remember how useful the puncuation is.

INTRIGUING ENDINGS

There is a mystery at the end of the poem. Something happened after the visitor was 'lifted over the threshold' to prevent the fire ever being lit again (and the house lived in, possibly).

- In your group, discuss possible explanations for this. What might have happened?

- Choose someone to play the part of the visitor, and someone to play the part of the person in the house. Take it in turns to put each in the *hot seat* in order to ask them questions about what happened and why things happened as they did.

You will need to think up good questions to ask, for example: 'Where had you come from?' or 'Tell us what you first saw and felt when you opened the door'.

You should try to build up a detailed picture of these two people: who they are, why they acted as they did; building up an account of what happened after the visitor was welcomed into the house. Make sure you relate your ideas to the clues given in the poem.

THE CHARGE OF THE LIGHT BRIGADE

I

Half a league, half a league,
  Half a league onward,
All in the valley of Death
  Rode the six hundred.
'Forward, the Light Brigade!
Charge for the guns!' he said:
Into the valley of Death
  Rode the six hundred.

II

'Forward, the Light Brigade!'-
Was there a man dismay'd?
Not tho' the soldier knew
  Some one had blunder'd:
Their's not to make reply,
Their's not to reason why,
Their's but to do and die:
Into the valley of Death
  Rode the six hundred.

III

Cannon to right of them,
Cannon to left of them,
Cannon in front of them
  Volley'd and thunder'd;
Storm'd at with shot and shell,
Boldly they rode and well,
Into the jaws of Death,
Into the mouth of Hell
  Rode the six hundred.

IV

Flash'd all their sabres bare,
Flash'd as they turn'd in air
Sabring the gunners there,
Charging an army, while
  All the world wonder'd:
Plunged in the battery-smoke
Right thro' the line they broke;
Cossack and Russian
Reel'd from the sabre-stroke
  Shatter'd and sunder'd.
Then they rode back, but not,
  Not the six hundred.

V

Cannon to right of them,
Cannon to left of them,
Cannon behind them
  Volley'd and thunder'd;
Storm'd at with shot and shell,
While horse and hero fell,
They that had fought so well
Came thro' the jaws of Death.
Back from the mouth of Hell,
All that was left of them,
  Left of six hundred.

VI

When can their glory fade?
O the wild charge they made!
  All the world wonder'd.
Honour the charge they made!
Honour the Light Brigade,
  Noble six hundred!

Alfred, Lord Tennyson

PUTTING IT ALL TOGETHER

The Charge of the Light Brigade celebrates the bravery of the British soldiers who died when they were mistakenly ordered to charge at the Russian soldiers in the Crimea in October 1854. They had no hope of staying alive so the poet makes us think deeply about the tragic waste of lives as the soldiers charged to certain death.

READING 'THE CHARGE OF THE LIGHT BRIGADE'

- First of all, read through this poem on your own and spend a few minutes writing about your first impressions, thoughts and feelings.

- As a class, stand or sit in a circle to read the poem. Take it in turns to read one line each, but join in altogether as a class for the last two lines of each verse. Make sure you put lots of expression into your voice: it is up to you to create the impression of the sounds of hundreds of horses galloping, shouts, cries, cannon shots, sword clanging. Try to keep the pace fast: the poet has helped you to do this by writing lots of short lines, and sometimes running one line into the next with no punctuation between them.

- Think carefully about the words you have to read. If one of your lines is a question, show this by the tone of your voice. Sometimes the poet helps you to know which words to emphasise by using alliteration, for example, 'shot and shell'. If one of your lines ends with an exclamation mark, think about the expression you will put in your voice.

- Having read it through once to get the 'feel' of the lines, go on to rehearse the class reading of the poem, including sound effects. Try reading it whilst walking round to create a sense of movement. If possible, invite another class or teacher to watch and listen while you perform your reading.

- When you have read the poem aloud and included some movement in your reading, discuss with your group the volume and the pace (speed) of sections of the poem. How does the poet control the pace and how does he suggest the volume?

- After your performance, compare the illustration of the poem with the poem itself. What impression of the charge does the picture give you? Is it the same impression that the poem gives? Which do you think is a more powerful way of describing the experience of the charge? Why?

POEMS FOR MANY VOICES

Read these two poems and consider what they gain from being read by several voices together.

They held up a stone.
I said, 'Stone.'
Smiling they said, 'Stone.'

They showed me a tree.
I said, 'Tree.'
Smiling they said, 'Tree.'

They shed a man's blood.
I said, 'Blood.'
Smiling they said, 'Paint.'

They shed a man's blood.
I said, 'Blood.'
Smiling they said, 'Paint.'

Dannie Abse, adapted from the Hebrew of Amir Gilboa

YOU!

You!
Your head is like a hollow drum.
You!
Your eyes are like balls of flame.
You!
Your ears are like fans for blowing fire.
You!
Your nostril is like a mouse's hole.
You!
Your mouth is like a lump of mud.
You!
Your hands are like drum-sticks.
You!
Your belly is like a pot of bad water.
You!
Your legs are like wooden posts.
You!
Your backside is like a mountain top.

Igbo, Nigeria

CHORAL SPEAKING

- Read aloud Dannie Abse's poem which comes from a collection of poems about war. Try reading it in the following ways: one voice reads the main part of the poem, *but*

  the whole class together reads the last word of each verse

  or

  one voice reads the last word in line two of each verse.

- What effect did hearing one voice saying a word have?

- Discuss with your group what the poem means.

- Read 'You'. Divide the class into two groups, and sit in two lines facing each other. One group should read the lines which say 'you'; the other group reads the other lines back. Then read it again, swapping roles. Think about changing over the lines which you read. Think about how to say the word 'You' – will it sound the same each time it is read?

- How do you think that the speaker feels about the person being spoken to in the poem and why?

- What effect does repeating the word 'you' have?

SUNNY MARKET SONG

1st Voice: Coffee
Spiced chocolate
Ackee

White yam
Yellow yam
Juicy melon

Breadfruit
Grapefruit
Arrowroot

2nd Voice: I want some cinnamon
and tamarind, mam

3rd Voice: Buy quatty wo't' noh, gal –
Buy quatty wo't'

1st Voice: Tapioca
Sarsaparilla
Cassava

Snapper fish
Fresh fish
Strong charcoal

Dry coconuts
Water coconuts
Mango

2nd Voice: I want some cloves and
lemon, mam

3rd Voice: Buy quatty wo't' noh, gal –
Buy quatty wo't'

1st Voice: Custard apple
Ripe pineapple
Sweet potatoes

Cho-cho
Callalu
Coco

Soursop
Sweetsop
Sorrel

2nd Voice: I want some nutmeg and
ginger, mam

3rd Voice: Buy quatty wo't' noh, gal –
Buy quatty wo't'

1st Voice: Foo-foo plantain
Ripe plantain
Pawpaw

Fever grass
Strong-back herb

Mount'n honey comb
Orange
Cabbage
Hominy corn

2nd Voice: I want some allspice and
pepper, mam

3rd Voice: Buy quatty wo't' noh, gal –
Buy quatty wo't'

1st Voice: Fresh whelks
Beeswax
Floor dye

Blackeye peas
Congo peas
Okra

Jackass rope
Raw sugar
Ripe bananas

2nd Voice: I want some scallion and
annatto, mam

3rd Voice: Buy quatty wo't' noh, gal –
Buy quatty wo't'

James Berry

For performance:
1st Voice represents general market voices
2nd Voice represents girl buying spices and seasoning
from 3rd Voice, the stallholder.

GLOSSARY   GLOSSARY   GLOSSARY   GLOSSARY

ackee	fruit
quatty	penny and a half, or three halfpennies
Buy quatty wo't' noh, gal	buy three halfpennies worth, won't you, lady
cassava	staple food
cho-cho	fruit of a climbing vine, eaten as a vegetable
callalu	edible leaves, greens
soursop/sweetsop	fruit
foo foo	doughy mashed plantain
okra	vegetable
jackass rope	rope made from twisted tobacco leaves
annatto	tree whose berries are used for dye

READING DRAMATIC POETRY

- As a class, rehearse a reading of 'Sunny Market Song'. The poet has offered you some advice about [how to] perform this poem. Divide the [class] into three groups: one group [is] responsible for '1st Voice', ano[ther] group for '2nd Voice' and the third group for '3rd Voice'. If you are [not] used to the Carribean dialect [the] glossary above will help yo[u]. [You might] include sound effects to fit the [market] scene.

- The third voice always says the sa[me] words; these lines are like a chor[us]. What effect did this have on you [when] you were reading or listening to t[he] lines? How does the poet make '1s[t] Voice' and '2nd Voice' sound different?

WHAT NEXT?

- In groups of four, use this planning route to choose, plan, rehearse and perform a selection of poetry. At each point, note what you have done in your journal. Comment on other groups' performances as well as your own.

1 **AUDIENCE** – Discuss possible audiences, for example infants, senior citizens at Christmas, parents, school assembly, or another class. You may not be able to perform for this audience, but having an audience in mind will help you to choose appropriate poems.

2 **THEME** – With your audience in mind, decide on a theme, for example the seasons, poems about sport, humorous poems, poems by one poet, poems written in a dialect such as a Scottish dialect, Cockney, or Jamaican.

3 **SEARCH** – Browse through as many poetry anthologies as you can. Read as many poems as possible. List poems you like which may be suitable for your group's presentation.

4 **SELECT** – Share your choice with the rest of the group. Together, make a selection of poems which will go together – perhaps some that are long and some short, some modern and some from centuries ago.

5 **ANNOTATE** – Read each of the chosen poems carefully and discuss it together. Copy the poems and annotate them – that is, make your notes around them to help you understand and perform the poem.

6 **PLAN** –

- who will read each poem
- how the performance will be introduced and concluded
- how you will move from one poem to the next (you may choose to link the poems using a narrator, or using movement or dance for example)
- whether you will use any simple costumes or masks.

7 **PRACTICE** – Rehearse reading the poems aloud. Listen to each other read and offer constructive advice, for example about pace, volume, pauses, expression in the voice, stressing certain words.

8 **PERFORM** – Present your group's performance to your class. If possible, go on to present it to the audience for whom you planned it.

9 **REFLECT** – After your performance, talk about it together. Did it go as planned? How did your audience react? Did you have enough material? Would you do it differently another time?